Carolina Catch

Sunburst Trout Farm

DEBBIE MOOSE

Carolina Catch

Cooking North Carolina Fish and Shellfish

FROM MOUNTAINS TO COAST

The University of North Carolina Press CHAPEL HILL

Publication of this book was supported in part by a generous gift from Cyndy and John O'Hara.

Text © 2018 Debbie Moose
Food photography © 2018 Juli Leonard
All rights reserved
Manufactured in the United States of America
Designed by Kimberly Bryant and set in Whitman
by Rebecca Evans

The University of North Carolina Press has been a member of the Green Press Initiative since 2003.

Cover illustration: Rainbow trout, © Studioimagen73 /istockphoto.com; oysters, © Jag-cz/stock.adobe.com. Seasonal icons © MaewChansilpa/istockphoto.com.

Library of Congress Cataloging-in-Publication Data
Names: Moose, Debbie, author.
Title: Carolina catch : cooking North Carolina fish and
       shellfish from mountains to coast / Debbie Moose.
Description: Chapel Hill : The University of North
       Carolina Press, [2018] | Includes index.
Identifiers: LCCN 2017044385 | ISBN 9781469640501
       (cloth : alk. paper) | ISBN 9781469640518 (ebook)
Subjects: LCSH: Cooking (Seafood)—North Carolina.
Classification: LCC TX747 .M775 2018 | DDC 641.6/92—
       dc23 LC record available at https://lccn.loc.gov
       /2017044385

To Rob, who's never shellfish and sometimes a little fishy

《《　》》

And to the people who work every day to bring the state's
abundant fish and shellfish to our tables

Contents

Appetizers

Soups and Salads

Main Dishes

Sides, Sauces, and Sassy Goodies

Profiles

Carolina Catch

Locals Seafood

Introduction

Celebrate the Bounty from the State's Waters, and Learn What You Can Do to Help Sustain It (Hint: Eat It!)

North Carolina is a very fishy state. It ranks near the top of coastal states in the number of fish species caught. Inland streams, ponds, and rivers increase the abundance. Aquaculture adds to the offerings with farmed trout, oysters, and even caviar. Whether you catch your own or prefer to drop a line in a well-stocked fish market, choices abound from the coast to the mountains.

For the first eighteen years of my life, I encountered fish primarily in stick form, which my mother regularly plopped on the dinner table. Then I experienced raw oysters and fried soft-shell crabs. They were nothing like those rectangular objects of my youth, and not just because they had natural shapes. The pure, oceany flavor, sweetness, and variety of North Carolina fish and seafood switched me on to it forever. Today, I grill tuna, steam shrimp, pan-sear mountain trout, and fry catfish. When I steam littleneck clams, I often savor them in pristine beauty—no butter or cocktail sauce, just the salty taste of the sea.

This book is a guide so that you, too, can explore the range of fish and shellfish that the state offers. Learn how to spot the best-quality fish and shellfish and about issues affecting your ability to get this natural resource on the table. There's information on storing and handling fish and seafood. And ways to make new choices that let you enjoy the full range of fish and shellfish. Profiles of those who bring the catch to us lucky eaters give a glimpse into the state's fishing history and the challenges watermen face today.

With so much to savor, move beyond the usual favorites to less familiar kinds of fish. Ever heard of dogfish, amberjack, or grunt? Those are admittedly odd names for delicious, versatile ocean fish. Inland, responsibly farmed trout, hybrid striped bass and catfish, and such wild-caught fish as spot and perch are great options. Recipes in this book offer a range of North Carolina fish alternatives to help you start exploring based on your current preferences. Use "Think Seasonal," a list of which fish are most abundant at different times of the year, with notes on their flavors and textures, to take advantage of the seasonality of fish and shellfish. "Think Seasonal" also helps you help overfished species by guiding you into the new waters of less familiar fish, which will quickly become mealtime favorites. Because this book focuses on fish and shellfish in North Carolina, you won't see recipes using fish such as salmon or halibut, and sea scallops are caught off the Virginia coast (although often by North Carolina boats). But the state offers plenty to enjoy.

Many people still have a fear of fish; they're afraid of overcooking it, undercooking it, or just plain messing it up. If you have this condition, you can overcome it. In "Best Basics," clear instructions explain classic cooking techniques from frying and broiling to grilling and poaching. Tips on selecting, handling, and freezing the catch ensure that you start with the best fish and shellfish. The biggest tip: purchase North Carolina fish and shellfish. You'll get the freshest product available, plus you'll support local economies and family fishermen who are facing growing challenges.

The main argument for using local fish or shellfish? It tastes darn good. So, welcome aboard to explore. You'll have a great trip.

Community and Culture

North Carolina's abundant fish and shellfish have not only fed people from the mountains to the coast for centuries but also have created special ways of life.

Numerous celebrations honor the catch in small communities across the state. There are too many festivals to list here (see the Department of Travel and Tourism's website, visitnc.com, for a full roster), but some interesting ones celebrate fish whose charms may not be obvious to the casual eater.

The Swansboro Mullet Festival in the eastern part of the state, which has been going since 1954, honors a small, oily fish with a strong flavor. The fish fed the workers who built a bridge that was a vital link for the community, so the town held a festival to celebrate the bridge and the mullet that helped make it possible.

In the mountain town of Cherokee, the spring Rainbow and Ramps

Festival celebrates the return of wild trout and the pungent onionlike wild greens. It marks the importance of trout to the Native American community.

Nearly fifty years ago, the Spot Festival in Hampstead took a fish that was available and widely enjoyed in eastern North Carolina and made it the center of a fish fry fund-raiser for the fire department. The festival has been going ever since. Spot is a small panfish usually served whole. Spot and croaker, another small panfish, are also popular in Lumbee communities around Robeson County.

For generations, fish frys have fed crowds for fund-raisers, church events, and family reunions. They have a special place in African American food history, according to *Soul Food: The Surprising Story of an American Cuisine One Plate at a Time*, by Adrian Miller. Miller writes that West Africans ate a lot of fish and enslaved people from that area brought fishing traditions with them. Slave owners considered fish, particularly catfish, to be inferior food and often used it to supplement slave rations. Poor whites also caught fish. It was humble but always available.

"As a person who grew up on the coast, I can say you talk to a seventy-five-year-old black man, or white man, they'll say fish and grits embody the coast here. Not shrimp and grits," says Keith Rhodes, chef at Catch restaurant in Wilmington. "Those two items were very inexpensive. A spot and a cup of grits, you can feed two people with that and you had access to it."

By the 1950s, fish was not a big part of most white Americans' diets, but black Americans were consuming a lot of it, especially the abundant inland catfish. In the 1960s and 1970s, African American churches cleaned up the reputation of fish frys, which had become rowdy social events, and began holding them to raise money for projects. The connection between African Americans and fish had become so strong, Miller writes, that the original ads for the McDonald's Filet-O-Fish sandwich targeted the community with lines like "Have a Saturday night fish fry."

Changes Affect What's on Your Plate

Seafood has sustained the economies of coastal towns for generations. Jan DeBlieu writes in "Hatteras Journal" about a 1944 harvest of spot at Salter Path. Men hauled in enough fish that, when sold, families could live on the money for a year: "Those baskets and truckloads of fish meant new dresses, new hats, new shoes, new curtains and a lot of other new things."

Much of that catch left the state, and a lot of the state's fish and shellfish still does. The established supply lines run north to New York and Baltimore, large cities where fishermen can be fairly certain of a good sale. According to Ann Simpson of N.C. Catch, the state's east to west sales routes are less robust despite population growth in the Piedmont and western North Carolina.

Also, the days of a single haul making a North Carolina fisherman's year are gone. Today, the issue isn't buying new curtains or shoes but being able to stay afloat at all.

The biggest problem: farmed seafood from other countries flooding U.S. markets. It's cheap and easy for large sellers such as supermarkets to order it in bulk, and seasonality doesn't come into play—popular varieties, especially shrimp, are available year-round. As much as 90 percent of shellfish and fish (wild caught and farm raised) consumed in the United States comes from overseas. However, some overseas seafood carries a well-documented price, including the use of preservatives, poorly regulated quality, environmental problems in overseas farming, and the use of slave labor in production and harvest.

As the North Carolina coast has become a popular vacation destination, land values have risen. Development pressures have forced many fish houses—where fishermen take their catch for processing and sale to markets—to close and the prime waterfront land they sit on is sold for condos or houses. In the past decade, about a third of coastal fish houses have closed, according to North Carolina Sea Grant. The shortage of fish houses means that fishermen must take longer trips, with larger fuel bills, to processors—and time is money for a perishable product. Losing a fish house also means losing the fishing village environment and history that tourists like to see.

Then there's fish politics. Talk to a fisherman, and you'll hear about government regulations that control when they're allowed to catch what varieties of seafood, types of equipment required, and kinds of records they must keep. The push-and-pull of environmental and overfishing concerns, which responsible fishermen share, with making a living means they have to deal with Raleigh or Washington, D.C., along with finding the fish. Most fishermen fish several kinds of fish and shellfish at different times, changing and maintaining expensive gear for each. Some augment incomes by traveling across the country to fish for salmon in Alaska during the summer, taking them away from their families.

Many consumers are unaware of these issues. But as arcane as fish politics can seem, they affect getting local fish and shellfish for your table. It's time to get informed and speak up.

"The public is one of the stakeholders in all this," says Hardy Plyler, an Ocracoke fisherman.

Give Some Love to Unfamiliar Fish

Popular fish such as flounder, snapper, and grouper are getting harder to find owing to overfishing, and their prices are increasing. So eating lesser-known fish makes both environmental and economic sense. They can be another source of income for fishermen as well. And they taste great.

Many of these species used to be called "trash fish" because they were by-catch—caught in the process of catching other fish. Fishermen used to throw them away because no one would buy them (although fishermen often ate them at home). But there's nothing trashy about these less familiar fish—they're good eating. Dogfish (also known as cape shark) is just as good as cod in fish and chips. In fact, much of the dogfish caught off North Carolina's coast ends up across the pond in Britain's famous fish and chips because of cod shortages. Sea mullet is a rich, flaky white ocean fish that bakes great in a sauce, beating the heck out of flounder. Tilefish is sweet and flaky, a fine substitute for snapper. Do you like salmon? Try amberjack. The texture of black drum is similar to grouper.

Locals Seafood

Locals Seafood

Chefs are exploring lesser known fish as companies like Locals Seafood in Raleigh, Salty Catch in Beaufort, and others are working to build supply lines going into the state instead of away from it. North Carolina Sea Grant in Raleigh works with restaurants to encourage chefs to use these fish. And as availability increases along with awareness of the need to use the full variety of fish the state offers, chefs are showing interest. Even lionfish, an invasive species that's threatening coastal fisheries, is showing up on menus.

Unlike overseas fish farming, the state's aquaculture industry is generally considered well regulated. "United States farm-raised fish is at a higher standard and most people are farming responsibly," says Ryan Speckman of Locals Seafood in Raleigh. He sells farmed trout, and catfish along with farm-raised clams and oysters.

There are efforts to produce farm-raised prawns and shrimp, which is the nation's most popular seafood. High-quality oysters and clams are being farmed on the coast. Trout farming has a long history in the mountains. "North Carolina is becoming the Napa Valley of oysters. A North Carolina oyster trail is being instituted to highlight oysters being culture-grown and wild caught. Masonboro, Cedar Island, Ocracoke. They're doing a wonder for our area," says chef Rhodes. "It's nice to have alternatives, especially when you think about the mountains and getting trout. Everybody is trying to think about how they can replenish supply."

What Consumers Can Do

One simple thing can make a difference: Ask for North Carolina fish and shellfish. Ask questions when you look at a menu or approach a fish counter, and make it clear that you prefer local fish and shellfish.

Explore lesser known fish. If you like a certain kind of fish—flounder, for example—start by asking a knowledgeable fishmonger for ones similar in texture and flavor. There are a lot of good fish in the sea, just like your mama always said.

Learn to cook fish properly. "There is a fear of fish because people still don't know how to cook it. People eat overcooked, dried-out fish and decide they don't like fish," says Wanchese fisherman Dewey Hemilright. "And broaden your brush with other kinds."

Be aware of fish politics, including regulatory and environmental issues that may affect fishermen's livelihoods and the ability to get local products. Remember that cheap overseas seafood can have a huge price, both locally and internationally. "The consumer can demand access to fresh local seafood. Educate yourself about the issues and contact your representatives. Educate yourself about the real cost of imports," says Hardy Plyler.

Learn More

North Carolina Sea Grant: Research and information on North Carolina fish and seafood; offers Local Catch guidelines. ncseagrant.ncsu.edu

N.C. Catch: Information and advocacy about issues affecting North Carolina fishermen. On the site are links to Brunswick Catch, Carteret Catch, Ocracoke Fresh, and Outer Banks Catch, which certify and label stores and restaurants that offer North Carolina fish and shellfish. nccatch.org

Marine Stewardship Council: Offers labeling for certified sustainable seafood and other information on making fish choices. www.msc.org

NOAA's Fishwatch: Information on the most popular fish and seafood raised or harvested in the United States and how to make informed choices. www.fishwatch.org

Whole Foods Market Responsibly Farmed: Considered a reliable label for farm-raised seafood.

Monterey Bay Aquarium's Seafood Watch: Offers nationwide guidelines and a mobile app to help with sustainable seafood choices. www .seafoodwatch.org

Dive into This Book

"Best Basics" offers clear instructions on selecting and prepping fish, popular cooking methods, and freezing the catch. When a recipe refers to "Best Basics," simply turn to that section for detailed instructions.

"Think Seasonal" is a guide to peak seasonal availability—times of year when specific fish and shellfish are most abundant. Notes on each fish offer information on its flavor and texture. All this is to help you select and enjoy less familiar fish in the recipes to follow or in your own recipes. Explore!

Most recipes include alternatives fish choices to help you as well.

Locals Seafood

Best Basics

Get Started

How to Pick Top-Quality Fish and Shellfish, and How to Treat It Right

SELECTING AND PURCHASING

Start by going to a reliable seller who specializes in local seafood. Be aware that fish and shellfish have peak seasons, like produce, and being familiar with seasonality can lessen the chances of purchasing poor-quality or mislabeled fish. If you see out-of-season fish at cheap prices, be careful. It may be an attempt to pass off frozen fish as fresh or a cheaper fish as a more expensive species.

Federal laws require most retailers, including supermarkets, to label seafood with the country of origin. Beyond that, labeling is a free-for-all. Some commonly used buzzwords are unregulated and therefore mean nothing—without set standards, they're just marketing terms. Those include "sustainable," "environmentally aware," and "natural."

Use smell, sight, and touch to pick out the best items. Keep purchases cold—markets should provide ice—in transit and when you get home.

Fish

Fish shouldn't smell fishy. Fresh fish have a clean, oceany smell. An off-odor or chemical-like smell might indicate that a preservative was used.

Whole fish should look moist and have clear markings and bright eyes. Sunken eyes, dull colors, and dry scales are signs that a fish is old. Fillets should appear opaque and moist with no discoloration on the edges, not slimy and dull.

Look for firm flesh that springs back from the touch. Fish shouldn't feel slick, which may indicate age or use of a preservative.

Shellfish

Fresh, uncooked shrimp is firm and doesn't have a strong odor. Don't buy shrimp that look soggy or mushy. Overseas farmed shrimp is often doused with preservatives and farmed under low environmental standards. A Pulitzer Prize–winning Associated Press series exposed the use of slave labor in Southeast Asian shrimp farming. So think twice before purchasing overseas shrimp: it costs more than you think.

Locals Seafood

Oysters and clams in the shell are alive, so handle them with special care. Don't purchase any that are open or that won't close tightly when the shell is tapped. Keep them on ice or in the refrigerator at all times, in a breathable container such as a paper bag, mesh bag. or burlap sack. (You need air to live, and so do they.) Use within a day or two. Shucked oysters are usually sold in glass jars or plastic containers. They should be fat and creamy gray, and the containers should not contain an excessive amount of oyster liquor. Keep refrigerated.

The legs of live crabs, including soft-shell crabs, should move a bit. Don't purchase crabs that appear to be dead. If you purchase cleaned fresh soft-shells that are no longer alive, ask if they were cleaned that day—otherwise, pass. It's safest to purchase them alive and clean them yourself (it's easy). Use hard crabs the same day you purchase them.

Crabmeat sold in plastic containers on ice, the kind you purchase at a fish market, is considered fresh even though it has been steamed or pasteurized—technically, it's cooked. It comes in jumbo lump or lump, backfin, and special. The difference is in the sizes of the pieces of crabmeat and the prices, with jumbo lump or lump being the largest and most expensive. Consider how you plan to use the crab when choosing the type. Crabmeat is extremely perishable. Check the sell-by date before buying, keep it refrigerated, and use within two or three days. There should be no odor when you open the container, and remove any stray bits of shell. Canned crabmeat, which doesn't require refrigeration, is generally of lower quality.

Tools

Fish spatula: Makes turning fillets while frying or lifting them from the grill much easier. (It's also great for stir-frying in a wok or lifting frittatas from the pan.)

Small needle-nose plier: Purchased from the hardware store and dedicated to kitchen use, this helps in removing stray bones in fillets before you cook.

Soft brush: Useful in removing fish scales.

Grill pans: These sit over the grill grate and keep flaky fish from falling through and keep smaller items like shrimp in place.

Oyster knife: With a short, flat blade and dull point, this is essential for opening shellfish. Look for a heavy one with a firmly attached handle. A clam knife, which has a longer, thinner blade to open the smaller shellfish, may also be helpful.

Heavy work gloves: To protect your hands while shelling oysters or clams.

Large, hand-held metal nutcrackers or specialized shell crackers: Good for opening the hard shells of steamed crabs.

Shrimp deveiners: Long, curved plastic tools that remove shells and veins at once. A small, sharp knife can be used for this purpose as well.

Sharp kitchen shears: For removing side fins of whole fish and cleaning soft-shell crabs.

Instant-read thermometer: To gauge the doneness of fish.

Freezing

If you find an abundance of fish or shellfish at a good price, it's easy to freeze it at home. A vacuum sealer is great, but regular freezer bags will also work fine. Be sure to label containers with the kind of seafood, date, and amount. Use within three to six months for the best flavor.

Fish fillets: Pat the flesh as dry as possible. Wrap each fillet tightly in heavy plastic wrap—this not only keeps out air but allows you to remove the number of fillets you need. Stack the wrapped fillets in a freezer bag, press out the air, and label.

Shrimp: Do not remove the shells, but do remove the heads, if attached. For short-term freezing, put the shrimp in a freezer bag and squeeze out as much air as possible. For longer-term freezing and to ensure against freezer burn, pack the shrimp in water, which will push out air. Put the shrimp in a plastic freezer container and add enough cold water to cover, leaving room for the water to expand as it freezes. Label the container.

Oysters and clams: These can be frozen in their shells, which has the added advantage of making them easy to open to use in soups and other cooked dishes. Rinse and scrub the shells under cold water to remove any dirt, then place in a heavy freezer bag. When thawing, open the shells in a bowl to catch their liquor.

Crab: For hard-shell crabs, cook and remove the meat before freezing it in an airtight container. Soft-shell crabs can be cleaned and then frozen raw. Wrap each one tightly in heavy plastic wrap, then stack in a freezer bag and press out as much air as possible. To freeze purchased crabmeat that is already steamed or pasteurized, put it in heavy freezer bags and squeeze out the air or use airtight containers. If the crabmeat is in the unopened container you purchased it in, place the container in a freezer bag.

Prep Time: Get the Catch Ready to Cook

CLEANING SOFT-SHELL CRABS

Soft-shell crabs should be cleaned just before cooking, no earlier. Using sharp kitchen shears, snip through the crab below the eyes and remove the face. Turn the crab over, then pull back and cut off the small triangular apron. Lift each side of the top shell and use a small knife to scrape out the gills, which are gray-white and finger-shaped. Rinse the crab well. Note: Yellow material you may see is harmless crab roe. Some people remove it because they think it tastes bitter.

DEVEINING SHRIMP

If using shelled shrimp in dishes, you may want to remove the black digestive tract (the vein), which goes down the shrimp's long side, away from the legs. This step is not necessary for safety but can be a personal preference. Remove the heads if the shrimp are not already headed. If using a deveiner, insert it along the long side of the shrimp, then push through to the tail and remove the shell. The vein will come out at the same time. If using a small paring knife, shell the shrimp first, then run the knife down the back to remove the vein. Rinse the shrimp well after deveining.

Scrub the fish with a soft brush under cold running water to remove scales. If the fish has not been gutted, slice open the belly from the head through the tail (leave half of the tail on each side; you'll need it). Remove anything inside, then rinse the fish inside and out in cold water and pat dry.

Place the fish on a stable surface, such as a counter or a cutting board that won't move around. Make a cut just behind the gills and remove the head. Turn the fish so that the head points away from you; never cut toward you. Using a sharp but flexible knife, grasp the tail and work the knife horizontally along the bottom of the top fillet toward the head, pulling the tail and top fillet up as you go. Try to follow the backbone. When you get to the end, the top fillet should come off easily. Place the top fillet on the cutting surface. Cut off the tail and use sharp kitchen shears to remove the side fins. Turn over the fish and repeat to get the bottom fillet.

Locals Seafood

Check the fillets for stray bones and remove them with needle-nose pliers.

Large, thick fish such as tuna, mackerel, or mahi are cut into steaks, but you're unlikely to deal with these big fish at home.

OPENING OYSTERS OR CLAMS

Protect the hand holding the raw shellfish with a heavy work glove. Insert an oyster knife at the front of the shell, opposite the hinge, and work your way around, twisting the knife to pry the shell open. Alternatively, insert the oyster knife at the hinge and twist.

Raw clams can be difficult to open. If you are planning to cook with the clam meat, the easiest way to open clams is to freeze them. After freezing, hold the clam under cold running water to thaw slightly, then insert a clam knife or table knife through the front of the shell and twist.

Cooking: Get Great Results Every Time

IS IT DONE YET?

This is the biggest question about cooking fish, and the answer depends on the kind of fish or shellfish being prepared. The most important thing to remember is not to overcook—the results will be dry and chewy. Go by feel or use an instant-read thermometer. For fish except tuna, the flesh should be flaky but moist at the thickest part of the fillet, with an internal temperature of 135° to 140°.

Think of tuna as a beefsteak. The flesh should be cooked to rare or medium, not completely through, or it will lose flavor and moisture. Rare, with a red center, is about 110°; medium, with a pink center, is about 115°.

Shrimp will turn bright pink and become fragrant when done. The shells of clams and oysters will pop open slightly. Whole crabs in the shell will turn bright red.

BOILING AND STEAMING

Shrimp, clams or oysters in the shell, whole crab, whole fish, and fish fillets.

Boiling and steaming are easy ways to prepare fish and seafood. Try using beer, white wine, or juice along with or instead of water. Add any combination of garlic, herbs, lemon slices, and seasoning blends, such as Old Bay. Cooking will take mere minutes, so watch your ingredients to avoid overcooking.

Boiling shrimp or whole hard crab: Use enough liquid to keep the items submerged. Bring the liquid and seasonings to a boil, then add the fish or shellfish. Boil shrimp just until it's bright pink and fragrant, from 3 to 5 minutes, depending on the size and amount. Drain. For crabs, bring enough liquid to cover the crabs along with any seasonings to a boil. Add the crabs, cover, and cook for 10 to 15 minutes or until they are bright red. Drain.

Steaming oysters: Before cooking, discard any oysters with open shells; they're unsafe to eat. Rinse the shells thoroughly to remove dirt. If the oysters are extremely muddy, rinse them outside using a garden hose. Steaming a lot of oysters can be messy, so get a large pot and a burner (such as a turkey fryer setup) and do it outdoors. Put 3 to 4 inches of water in the pot, then place the oysters in the basket section of the pot. Bring the water to a boil and steam for 8 to 10 minutes. As soon as the oysters begin to open, they are done and can be removed. Not all may cook at the same rate. If you're steaming only a half-dozen or so oysters, a steamer basket on the stove indoors will work.

Steaming clams: Before cooking, discard any clams with open shells; they're unsafe to eat. Clams can be steamed in a pan or in the oven. To pan-steam, place about an inch of liquid and desired seasonings in a wide sauté pan and bring to a boil. Add the clams, reduce the heat to a strong simmer, and cover the pan. Shake the pan occasionally to distribute the clams for even cooking. When the shells open, the clams are cooked; remove these as the rest continue to steam. Discard any shells that do not open after several minutes of cooking time for safety. Oven-steaming doesn't dilute the liquid the clams give off. Preheat the oven to 350°. Rinse the clams, place them in a rimmed baking pan, and cover the pan with foil. Bake for 10 to 15 minutes or until the shells pop open.

Steaming fish: Use this method with either whole fish or fillets. Whole fish will take longer. Place the fish on a rack or in a steamer basket (depending on its size) over a pot of boiling water. Cover with a lid or foil and steam until the fish tests done, about 10 minutes.

BROILING

Medium-thick fillets.

Putting fish under the intense, dry heat of an oven broiler raises the specter of overcooking. But if you keep an eye on it and use the right kind of fish, broiling is a quick way to a good meal.

Don't use thin fillets; they're too easy to overcook. Select fillets that are closer to 1 inch thick or more. Always top with a fat such as butter or olive oil to keep the fish moist. Position the oven rack near to the broiler. The cooking time will be a mere 5 to 8 minutes (depending on the thickness), so don't wander off. A sauce or topping usually enhances broiled fish.

CURING

Higher-oil fish such as bluefish, mackerel, swordfish, and trout.

Many people are familiar with gravlax, salmon cured in a combination of salt, sugar, and herbs or seasonings. But curing isn't limited to salmon—it works for other fish, too..

Use thin to medium-thin fillets, not thick steaks or whole fish. Remove all bones from the fillet but leave the skin on. Place the fillet on a piece of plastic wrap. Moisten the fillet lightly with vodka or sake, if desired. For every pound of fish, stir together a mixture of 8 teaspoons of kosher salt and 4 teaspoons of sugar. You can add fresh herbs (dill is traditional) or other seasonings to the mixture. Four teaspoons of Japanese togarashi spice blend will add an interestingly spicy twist.

Rub the salt mixture over both sides of the fillet. Wrap tightly and place in a plastic container to hold moisture that escapes. Place the container in the refrigerator for 2 to 3 days, turning the fish over a couple of times.

Curing time depends on the thickness of the fillet. Check thin fillets after 2 days, thicker ones after 2½ days. When it feels firm to the touch and has no overly moist, raw appearance, the fish is cured. There should be no raw fish smell. The fillet should not be rubbery, a sign of overcuring.

To serve, slice the cured fillet thinly with a sharp knife.

FRYING AND SAUTÉING

Shelled oysters, peeled shrimp, fish, and soft-shell crab.

Frying

Debbie Moose

Two common ways to fry seafood are pan-frying and deep-frying. Pan-frying uses a pan with a relatively small amount of oil and the seafood is not completely submerged. Deep-frying uses a large pot or fryer with enough oil to submerge the fish. Pan-frying in about 1½ inches of oil, more traditional in the South, usually involves dredging the seafood in a light coating, often cornmeal-based. For batter-dipped fish—think fish and chips or tempura—deep-frying in 3 to 4 inches of oil (or more, depending on how much you're frying) is more common.

In either method, maintaining the proper oil temperature is crucial for crispy results. Keep track of the temperature with an instant-read thermometer, or use an electric frying pan or electric deep-fryer with a reliable temperature setting. Keep the oil at 375°, adjusting as you add and remove seafood.

Clean oil is important to prevent the fish and shellfish from burning. If breading or batter falls off as you fry, scoop it out with a small strainer and discard. If you are frying several batches and debris in the bottom of the pan or pot begins to burn, start over with fresh oil and a clean vessel.

Sautéing

Unlike other kinds of frying, when sautéing you cook quickly on medium-high heat in a small amount of fat with no or little breading, so that the seafood browns lightly. Use just enough oil or butter to coat the bottom of the pan. For fish, turn each piece only once.

FILLETING WHOLE COOKED FISH

Any whole finfish.

Place the cooked fish so that the tail is to your left and the head to the right. Use a knife and large spoon to pull out and remove the fin bones, if the fins were still attached. They should come out easily. Cut the top fillet where it meets the head and collar, through the skin and meat to the backbone. Cut through the skin and fillet where it meets the tail, but don't cut through the tail. Cut lengthwise through the center of the top fillet and pull it away in two pieces. (It may come off in one piece.) Remove the pieces of the top fillet to a plate. Check for stray bones.

Remove any seasonings you placed inside the fish while it was cooking (they may already have fallen out). Grasp the tail and gently pull the spine and skeleton up and away from the bottom fillet. The head should come with it; if not, remove it separately. Use the spoon and knife to check for and remove any stray bones from the bottom fillet, then place it on the plate with the other fillets.

GRILLING

Shrimp (in the shell or peeled), fish steaks, medium-thick fish, whole fish, and soft-shell crab.

Grilling fish and seafood is as easy as grilling burgers, as long as you watch out for a couple of things. Oil the grill grate or grill pan well to prevent the fish from sticking. Don't overcook the fish. It won't take as long as meats—a couple of minutes a side, depending on the thickness and the heat of the grill—so stay near the grill and turn the fish only once to keep it from falling apart. Fish and seafood are done when they are opaque and flaky. If you want to cook tuna to rare (110°), use an instant-read thermometer or insert the tip of a sharp knife to gauge the doneness you desire.

If grilling a whole fish, try a fish basket, which holds the fish together, or a grill pan with smaller slats than the grill grate. A grill pan is helpful for grilling shrimp and soft-shell crabs, too.

For a smoky flavor, purchase planks of cedar, alder, or other woods to use on the grill. Soak the planks well in water—at least 30 minutes—before placing them on the grill and putting the fish on top.

Briefly marinating fish before grilling adds flavor and helps it remain moist. Try soaking fillets or steaks for 15 to 20 minutes in a vinaigrette of olive oil, citrus juices, salt, and pepper, turning occasionally.

POACHING

Thick or medium-thick fish fillets and steaks.

Poaching is a gentle way to cook fish. Most people think of salmon for poaching, but any thick to medium-thick fish does well, and it's especially good for higher-oil varieties.

Flavor in the liquid will add flavor to the result. White wine is traditional, but also consider juice, broth, or beer. Poaching in buttermilk adds a tart flavor and makes the fish more tender. For something completely different and rich-tasting, poach in olive oil or butter.

Use a deep frying pan. Add enough liquid to cover the fish. Bring to a boil and add seasonings. Note: If you're poaching in olive oil, use only low to medium heat and monitor the temperature until the oil reaches 120°; don't let it boil.

Use a fish spatula to slip the fish gently into the liquid. Reduce the heat so that the liquid maintains a shimmer or shiver, not a boil. Depending on the thickness of the fillet or steak, cook for 2 to 8 minutes or until the fish tests done. (Poaching in olive oil may take longer.) Remove the fish to a platter and keep warm until serving; don't let it remain in the liquid or it may overcook.

ROASTING AND BAKING

Medium-thick to meaty fish fillets and whole fish.

Roasting a whole fish results in tender, moist meat with little effort. Medium-thick and meaty fillets can be roasted, too, but use a sauce, butter, or marinade to keep them from drying out. Either roast the fish directly on an oiled baking sheet, or wrap fillets in foil or parchment paper, add seasonings and lemon juice or wine, and then seal and roast the packets on a baking sheet.

Use a 400° to 425° oven. Whole fish will take longer to cook than fillets, which will be ready in 10 to 20 minutes, depending on the thickness. Watch carefully, and don't overcook. See "Best Basics," page 17, for instructions on carving cooked whole fish.

SMOKING

Debbie Moose

Higher-oil fish such as bluefish, mackerel, striped mullet, swordfish, and trout.

Smoking works best for fish with a higher oil content because the oil helps the smoke penetrate the meat while keeping fish moist over a long cooking time. You can smoke leaner kinds of fish, but you may want to use a marinade or oil, or brine the fish first, to prevent drying.

Follow your smoker's set-up directions. If you don't have a special smoker, a covered charcoal or gas grill will work.

If using a covered grill, set it up for indirect cooking. Soak a couple of good-size handfuls of wood chips in water for at least an hour. Pecan, apple, and hickory are good choices. Follow your grill's directions for adding the soaked chips to the grill. If you're using charcoal, when the coals are ready you can place the chips directly on the coals, but have water ready in case they flare up. You don't want flames. You can also put the soaked chips in an aluminum pan with a small amount of water and place the pan in the center of the grill, beneath where the fish will be. The heat inside the grill will cause them to smoke.

If you're smoking a large amount of fish, put more chips in to soak, and heat additional charcoal if you're using a charcoal grill.

Place the fish on an oiled grate or grill pan and place it in the grill or smoker. Make sure the fish is not directly over the heat. Cover the grill and smoke the fish for 50 to 60 minutes per pound, depending on the thickness of the fish. Steaks will take longer than thin fillets. Adjust the air vents to keep the temperature inside the grill at 200° to 250°. Check the grill's thermometer every 15 or 20 minutes to see that the temperature is correct, but keep the grill covered and the smoke inside as much as possible. Replenish wood chips and charcoal, if necessary.

At the end of the minimum cooking time, use an instant-read thermometer to test for doneness. The internal temperature of the fish should be 140° to 145°.

The flavor will intensify with time, so store the fish in the refrigerator and use it the next day for stronger smokiness. You can also wrap the smoked fish in airtight plastic bags and freeze it.

Fish fillets and shrimp.

The term is French for "under vacuum," and restaurant kitchens have used this method for decades. Food is sealed in a bag and cooked in a water bath that's held to a precise temperature. The method cooks food very evenly while retaining moisture, and you get a tender result. Because the food can't get hotter than the temperature of the water it's in, there's no overcooking. And you can add seasonings to the bag.

The first home sous-vide machines were expensive and large. Now several brands of compact home versions come at lower prices. Most provide cooking instructions.

Sous vide works well for seafood because it's very difficult to overcook with this method if you set the right temperature (the equipment comes with instructions and there are online resources). The only drawback is that a tuna steak won't have a seared crust. But after the tuna is cooked, quick-sear it in a very hot frying pan (just seconds on each side) to get that crunch.

Think Seasonal

Many people don't realize that wild-caught fish and shellfish, like fruits and vegetables, have seasonal peak availabilities. Learn what's plentiful throughout the year, and you'll get the freshest, best-tasting seafood—you might save a little money, too. Be aware of the most common farmed seafood, which is available year-round.

Here are kinds of North Carolina wild-caught fish and shellfish that you're most likely to find in fish markets, marked with a symbol or symbols indicating their peak season(s). The fish and seafood may also be available at other times, and a species may have more than one peak season. Also, commercial fishermen are subject to state restrictions on where and when they can fish, and the catch can be subject to weather conditions.

Each fish has notes on its flavor and texture to help you select the right ones for your recipes and inspire you to try new types of fish.

The list was compiled with information from North Carolina Sea Grant, Locals Seafood, and the N.C. Wildlife Federation.

Find the Best Fish and Seafood Year-Round

❄ WINTER

🌱 SPRING

☀ SUMMER

🍂 FALL

WILD-CAUGHT FISH

Amberjack	If you like salmon or swordfish, try this thick, juicy fish. Good for baking or roasting.	🌱 ☀
Bluefish	High oil content and assertive flavor. Be sure it's ultrafresh for best taste. Good smoked or grilled.	🌱 ☀
Catfish	Flaky, not as mild as farm-raised catfish, but a fine alternative to snapper.	❄

Cobia	Thick, meaty texture. Good for grilling and as a substitute for mahi or swordfish.	☾ ☀
Croaker	Medium-flavored, usually sold whole. Good fried.	☾ ☀
Dogfish (also called cape shark)	Meaty and thick with a mild flavor. Good for any preparation, especially fish and chips.	☀
Drum	Firm and meaty, with a mild flavor. Holds its shape well when cut in chunks. Good substitute for mahi.	☾
Flounder	The one fish most people like. Extremely mild, delicate, and flaky.	☾ ☀
Grouper	Popular for its very mild flavor and meaty texture.	☾ ☀
Grunt	White and flaky.	☾ ☀
Jumping mullet (also called fat mullet or striped mullet) and mullet roe	Earthy flavor, high oil content, and flaky texture. The roe is typically fried.	☾
Mackerel	Rich flavor, higher oil content, firm steaklike texture.	☾
Mahi	Popular favorite, but easy to over-cook and dry out. Steaklike texture.	☾
Monkfish	Firm texture and sweet flavor. Good substitute for grouper. Slices well and holds its shape while cooking. Good in soups or stews.	☀ ☾

Perch	Mild and flaky, similar to flounder.	◐ ✦
Pompano	Firm texture and sweet, buttery flavor. Good substitute for grouper.	✦
Porgy	Flaky, tastes similar to snapper.	✦ ◑
Rosefish	Light pink color, sweet, and firm. Cooks well whole. Good substitute for sea bass or snapper.	✦
Sea bass	Delightful, sweet flavor and great flaky texture. Good roasted whole.	◐ ✦
Sea mullet	Not the same as jumping mullet. Medium flavor and flaky texture. Good for baking or roasting with a sauce.	◐ ✦
Sea trout	Medium to mild, depending on species, with a flaky to firm texture.	◐ ✦
Shad and shad roe	Bony with an earthy, assertive flavor. Usually baked. The roe is prized.	◑
Sheepshead	Great all-around fish for baking or roasting in a sauce, pan searing, or frying. White and flaky, firm, and medium-thick, with a mild, sweet flavor.	◐
Snapper	Popular for its mild, sweet flavor and tender texture.	◑ ✦
Speckled, brown, and brook trout	Thin and flaky, with a medium flavor.	◐

Spot	Small, usually sold whole. Rich buttery flavor.	
Striped bass (also called rockfish)	Firm, with a mild flavor similar to sea bass.	
Swordfish	Medium-rich flavor and steaklike texture. Good for grilling or smoking.	
Tilefish	White, thin, flaky, and sweet. Good substitute for flounder or snapper.	
Triggerfish	Medium-thick, flaky, and sweet. Good substitute for flounder or snapper.	
Tuna and yellowfin tuna	The fish version of a filet mignon, with a meaty vibe. Best cooked rare, not all the way through.	

WILD-CAUGHT SHELLFISH

Clams	
Crab	
Oysters	
Shrimp	
Soft-shell crab	

THINK SEASONAL

(available year-round except where noted)

Catfish	Mild, medium-textured, and versatile. Good all around.
Clams	
Crawfish	
Oysters	
Rainbow trout	Medium flavor, flaky, and versatile, with a lovely pink color. Good substitute for snapper or flounder. Smokes and cures well.
Sturgeon	Very meaty. Good smoked.

Locals Seafood

Appetizers

»»

Tuna Crudo

Both Japanese sashimi and Italian crudo are raw fish dishes, but crudo includes juices, herbs, and other ingredients to accent the superfresh fish. Use the ingredients you prefer, but in general look for a citrus component, a fresh herb of some kind, and a hint of heat. Use good-quality olive oil—flavor counts—and it's a great time to break out the fancy salt.

ALTERNATIVES: trout, bass, snapper

Makes 4 servings

½ pound extremely fresh tuna

8 teaspoons fresh lemon juice, divided

Very good olive oil

Sea salt

1 red or green serrano pepper, very thinly sliced and seeded, divided

About 2 tablespoons very thinly sliced red onion, divided

About 2 tablespoons very thinly sliced fresh basil or sorrel, divided

Place 4 small appetizer plates in the refrigerator to chill. While the plates chill, use a sharp knife to cut the tuna into thin slices, about ¼ inch thick. Cut with the grain of the fish. Remove and discard any tough sinew or dark blood spots.

Spread 2 teaspoons of the lemon juice on the bottom of each chilled plate. Arrange 3 to 4 slices of tuna on top of the lemon juice. A fan pattern looks nice. Drizzle olive oil over the tuna. Sprinkle with salt.

Add serrano pepper slices as desired to each plate, then do the same with the red onions. Top with the basil or sorrel.

Cover the plates tightly with plastic wrap and refrigerate until immediately before serving. Do not refrigerate longer than about 20 minutes, or the lemon juice will begin to discolor the fish.

Bacon-Wrapped Mahi Bites

ALTERNATIVES:
monkfish, wahoo, drum

Makes 12 bites

Bacon-wrapped water chestnuts were the height of hors d'oeuvre achievement in the 1950s and 1960s. This version uses the good stuff—chunks of fresh fish. Sweet, complex sorghum syrup is less bitter than molasses.

6 slices bacon, cut in half
1 pound skinless mahi fillets, cut into 12 (1-inch) chunks
Salt
12 to 24 pieces pickled ginger, drained
12 (1-inch) pieces yellow or red bell pepper
Sorghum syrup or honey

Preheat the oven to 400°. Place half a strip of bacon on a cutting board. Place a chunk of mahi in the center and sprinkle lightly with salt. Top with 1 or 2 pieces of ginger, depending on the size of the pieces, and 1 piece of bell pepper. Wrap the ends of the bacon around it all and secure with a toothpick through the center. Repeat with the remaining mahi, ginger, bell peppers, and bacon.

Place the wrapped bundles on a rimmed baking pan and bake for 10 to 15 minutes, until the fish is cooked through and the bacon is slightly crisp.

Remove the bites to a serving plate. While still warm, drizzle lightly with sorghum syrup or honey. Serve warm.

Seafood Stuffed Peppers

A backyard crop of poblano peppers and summer corn from the farmers' market inspired this recipe, a variation on Mexican chiles rellenos. Coarsely chopped cooked shrimp would also be good, either alone or in combination with the fish, which you can cook however you prefer. Poblanos can have some heat; for a milder flavor, substitute Anaheim chiles.

ALTERNATIVES:
tuna, cobia, drum, shrimp

Makes 8 servings

8 medium-size fresh poblano peppers

Olive oil

2 to 3 ears fresh corn, enough to yield 1 cup fresh corn kernels

1 pound cooked sea bass

½ cup cooked black beans

3 tablespoons chopped red onion

¼ cup chopped cilantro

¼ cup plus 2 tablespoons shredded Monterey Jack cheese, divided

Salt, to taste

Sour cream for serving (optional)

Preheat the broiler and rub the peppers liberally with olive oil. Place the peppers on a baking sheet and broil, turning several times with tongs, until they are blistered all over. Place the hot peppers in a plastic bag and seal until the skin peels off easily, about 15 to 20 minutes. Remove stems and seeds from the peppers by slicing off the tops, but leave the peppers whole. Set aside.

Prepare a gas or charcoal grill for direct cooking or use a well-oiled stovetop grill pan indoors. Grill the corn, turning several times, for 4 to 5 minutes or until lightly toasted. Let cool, then use a small knife to scrape off the kernels into a large bowl.

Cut or pull the fish into chunks; don't make the pieces too small. Add the fish to the corn along with the black beans, red onions, cilantro, and ¼ cup of the cheese. Add salt to taste, then toss gently to combine the ingredients.

Preheat the oven to 350°. Use a small spoon to stuff the filling gently into the peppers, then place them on a nonstick baking pan. Try not to tear the peppers, but if one should tear, place the torn side facing the pan. Sprinkle the remaining cheese over the peppers. Cover the pan and bake for 30 minutes. Serve with sour cream if desired.

Smoked Swordfish with Creamy Lemon Drizzle

ALTERNATIVES:
smoked trout,
smoked bluefish,
smoked mackerel

Makes 12 to
20 servings,
depending on
serving method

Smoked fish has so much flavor that you can put it on a plate by itself and call it an appetizer. Add a tart drizzle and you have a nice foil for the richly flavored swordfish. You can make the drizzle a day ahead. Smoke the fish anytime and freeze it, then you're ready to make a quick appetizer.

2 pounds boneless, skinless swordfish steaks

¼ cup yogurt

½ cup sour cream

2 tablespoons fresh lemon juice

Salt and black pepper, to taste

½ teaspoon grated lemon zest

2 tablespoons chopped fresh parsley, plus sprigs for garnish

Crackers or toasted baguette slices for serving (optional)

See directions for smoking fish in "Best Basics," page 19.

Prepare the drizzle: In a small bowl, whisk together the yogurt, sour cream, lemon juice, salt, and pepper until the mixture is combined. Stir in the lemon zest and parsley. Cover and refrigerate until serving.

To serve, make sure that the fish is at room temperature or chilled, not hot off the smoker. Cut it into thin slices, arrange 2 or 3 slices on each of 12 appetizer plates, drizzle the sauce lightly over the slices, and garnish with parsley sprigs. Offer extra drizzle on the side. Or place slices of fish on crackers or toasted baguette slices, add drizzle, and arrange on a serving tray.

Fresh Corn and Trout Fritters

When fresh corn season arrives, I use it in every way possible. These patties make a good appetizer or light main dish. For a crunchy variation, substitute cornmeal for some or all of the flour. Be aware that the moist corn may spatter while cooking.

ALTERNATIVES:
catfish, flounder, striped bass, shrimp

Makes 8 to 10 servings

2 cups fresh corn kernels

½ cup chopped green bell pepper

½ cup chopped green onion

2 tablespoons all-purpose flour

¼ teaspoon chili powder

¼ teaspoon paprika

½ teaspoon salt

½ to ¾ pound skinless trout fillets, finely chopped

2 eggs, lightly beaten

Vegetable oil for frying

Place the corn, bell peppers, green onions, flour, chili powder, paprika, salt, and trout in a large bowl. Toss to combine. Stir in the eggs.

Put enough oil in a frying pan to come about 1 inch up the sides. Heat over medium until the oil shimmers. (See frying tips in "Best Basics," page 16.) Use 2 large spoons to scoop out the batter as patties and place them in the hot oil. Lightly press each patty to flatten it. Cook the patties, turning once, until they are brown on both sides. Drain them on paper towels or on a cooling rack placed over a plate. Keep the cooked patties warm in an oven on low heat until all the patties are cooked.

Smoked Trout Cheese Spread

ALTERNATIVES:
smoked bluefish
(stronger flavor)

Makes 10 to 12
servings

Smoked trout tastes milder than some smoked fish, which makes it a crowd pleaser. Briny capers and sharp red onions, along with a generous amount of black pepper, balance the rich cream cheese. The spread can be made up to 2 days before serving.

16 ounces cream cheese, at room temperature

2 tablespoons mayonnaise

¾ cup coarsely chopped smoked trout

¼ cup coarsely chopped red onion

Black pepper, to taste

2 tablespoons capers

½ cup chopped fresh parsley

Crackers for serving

Purchase smoked North Carolina trout or see directions for smoking fish in "Best Basics," page 19.

Put the cream cheese, mayonnaise, and smoked trout in the bowl of a food processor. Process until combined. Add the red onions, pepper, and capers, and pulse a few times until they are just mixed in.

Scrape the mixture into a container and sprinkle with the parsley. Cover and refrigerate for at least 8 hours or overnight. Serve with crackers.

Smoked Trout Deviled Eggs

ALTERNATIVES:
smoked mackerel,
smoked bluefish
(stronger flavor)

Makes 12
egg halves

Deviled eggs are always the first thing to go at potlucks and dinners, and adding North Carolina smoked trout to them will be a surprise. You can make these a day ahead and refrigerate, but know that the smoke flavor will intensify.

6 eggs

2 tablespoons sour cream

2 teaspoons whipped cream cheese

1 teaspoon Dijon mustard

2 tablespoons chopped smoked trout

Salt and black pepper, to taste

Chopped fresh chives for garnish

Purchase smoked North Carolina trout or see directions for smoking fish in "Best Basics," page 19.

Place the eggs in a saucepan, cover them with cold water, and place the pan over high heat. When the water comes to a boil, remove the pan from the heat and cover it with a lid. Let it sit 15 minutes, then drain and rinse the eggs under cold running water to stop the cooking process.

Peel the eggs and cut them in half lengthwise. Place the yolks in a medium-size bowl and mash them lightly with a fork. Add the sour cream, cream cheese, mustard, and trout. Stir to combine. Taste, then season with salt and pepper. Fill the whites evenly with the yolk mixture and garnish with chopped chives. Cover and refrigerate if not serving immediately.

Seafood Frittata

Frittatas aren't as well known as omelets, their French cousins, but I prefer to make frittatas because they're so simple. Just put the toppings on the eggs and pop the pan under the broiler: no flipping and folding. Frittatas are good ways to use leftover cooked shrimp or fish, along with your favorite vegetables and herbs. I've served them at breakfast, as a light lunch, or, cut into small wedges, as appetizers. Use plenty of olive oil so that the frittata won't stick to the pan.

Makes 8 servings

About ¼ cup olive oil

3 tablespoons chopped white or yellow onion

1 cup fresh spinach

8 eggs, well beaten

½ cup cherry tomato halves

Salt and black pepper, to taste

¼ to ½ cup coarsely chopped, cooked, skinless fish,
    cooked shelled shrimp, or both

Chopped fresh basil and/or shredded Parmesan cheese,
    optional

Place a large, oven-safe sauté pan with rounded sides over medium heat and add enough olive oil to cover the bottom. Add the onions to the hot oil and cook, stirring, until they begin to soften, then add the spinach. Cook, stirring, for 2 minutes or until the spinach is wilted.

Gently pour in the beaten eggs, distributing them evenly over the spinach and onions. Sprinkle on the cherry tomatoes, then season with salt and pepper. Distribute the cooked fish and/or shrimp on the frittata, letting the pieces nestle into the mixture. Cook the frittata until it begins to set around the edges but is still liquid in the middle.

Preheat the broiler to high. Remove the sauté pan from the stove and put it under the broiler. Broil until the frittata is set in the center and slightly browned; this will take just a few minutes, so watch carefully.

Remove the pan from the oven and use a slotted or fish spatula to remove the frittata to a serving plate. Let any excess olive oil drip back into the pan. Sprinkle the frittata with the optional basil and/or Parmesan, if using, and cut into 8 wedges. Serve warm or at room temperature.

Mini Crab Cakes with Mustard-Caper Sauce

I took these miniature goodies to a friend's birthday party, and they disappeared in minutes. Either warm or at room temperature, these little crab cakes taste great and look great, too. Serve them with sauce on the side for guests to add as they wish. If there are leftovers—a rare occurrence in my house—serve the cakes on a salad the next day.

Makes about 12

FOR THE SAUCE

1 cup mayonnaise

2½ tablespoons Creole mustard

½ teaspoon fresh lemon juice

½ teaspoon black pepper

1 tablespoon coarsely chopped capers

FOR THE CRAB CAKES

2 eggs

1 teaspoon fresh lemon juice

1 teaspoon Dijon or Creole mustard

½ teaspoon Worcestershire sauce

1 pound lump crabmeat

About 1 cup dry unseasoned bread crumbs, divided

1 tablespoon chopped fresh chives, plus more for garnish

Olive oil for frying

Up to 4 hours before serving, prepare the sauce. In a small bowl, mix together the mayonnaise, mustard, lemon juice, and pepper. Drain and rinse the capers well before coarsely chopping them and stirring them into the sauce. Cover and refrigerate.

Two to 3 hours before cooking, begin preparing the crab cakes. In a large bowl, stir together the eggs, lemon juice, mustard, and Worcestershire sauce. Gently stir in the crabmeat, ½ cup of the bread crumbs, and 1 tablespoon chives.

Sprinkle about ¼ cup of the remaining bread crumbs on a rimmed baking sheet. To mold the cakes, gently scoop the crab mixture into a ¼-cup measuring cup. Pack firmly but don't mash the mixture. Invert the cup onto the baking sheet. Continue until you have used all the crab mixture. Sprinkle the cakes with the remaining bread crumbs. Cover the cakes with plastic wrap and refrigerate for at least 2 hours.

Place a large sauté pan over medium heat and add enough olive oil to cover the bottom. When the oil is hot, add the crab cakes. Cook for about 3 minutes or until the bottoms of the cakes are brown. Use a spatula to turn the cakes over gently, trying to hold them together. Lower the heat if necessary to keep the cakes from overbrowning. Continue to cook until the other sides of the cakes are brown. Remove the cakes from the pan and drain them on a wire rack or on paper towels. Depending on the size of your sauté pan, you may need to work in batches.

To serve, place the crab cakes on a platter and sprinkle with chopped chives. Place the sauce in a bowl on the side.

Crunchy Lemon Shrimp

Tart and crisp, these taste like fried shrimp but without the mess and oil. Flat fish fillets, such as tilefish, trout, striped bass, or flounder, would be great, too.

Makes 4 to 6 servings

1½ cups panko
1 tablespoon chopped fresh chives
1 tablespoon grated lemon zest (about 1 lemon)
¾ teaspoon coarsely ground black pepper
½ teaspoon salt
1 cup all-purpose flour
2 eggs
28 large shrimp, peeled (deveined if desired)
Fresh Tartar Sauce (page 165)

Preheat the oven to 375°. Place a rack over a rimmed baking sheet and spray the rack with nonstick cooking spray.

In a shallow bowl, combine the panko, chives, lemon zest, pepper, and salt. Put the flour in a small bowl. Place the eggs in another small bowl and lightly beat.

Dip each shrimp one at a time in the flour and shake off the excess, then dip it in the egg and roll it in the panko mixture. Place the shrimp on the rack.

Bake for 10 minutes or until the shrimp are cooked through and the panko is lightly browned. Serve with Fresh Tartar Sauce.

Dewey's Baked Clams

Makes 6 servings

Dewey Hemilright has been fishing out of Wanchese for more than two decades, and he's as good at cooking coastal seafood as he is at catching it. As we sat in his boat on a fall day, he related his favorite clam recipe—which he'd never written down. This is my version, which is pretty close to what he told me except that I use Parmesan cheese instead of grated mozzarella. These clams prep fast, making them excellent snacks to put out while the rest of the meal is cooking. Figure on about three clams per person and multiply the recipe to suit your crowd.

18 littleneck clams, rinsed well

9 tablespoons Italian seasoned bread crumbs, divided

Unsalted butter

3 slices bacon, cut into 1½- to 2-inch pieces

Grated Parmesan cheese

Hot pepper sauce (such as Tabasco or Texas Pete), to taste

Preheat the oven to 350°. Open the clams, discard the top shells, and place the shells with the clams and their juices in a baking pan. (For tips on opening raw clams, see "Best Basics," page 13.)

Sprinkle ½ teaspoon of the bread crumbs on each clam, followed by a dot of butter and 1 piece of bacon. Bake for 15 to 20 minutes or until the bacon is cooked. Top the clams with a little Parmesan and a few drops of hot pepper sauce, then return to the oven for 2 to 3 more minutes or until the cheese is melted and lightly browned.

Dewey Hemilright, Wanchese

EDUCATING, ADVOCATING, PROTECTING

Dewey Hemilright has a message for North Carolinians: It's your coast and your seafood. Eat it.

"I want consumers to demand fresh, local seafood. This resource is owned by the people of North Carolina," he says. "We are really blessed here."

Hemilright grew up in Wanchese and started fishing more than twenty years ago after deciding college wasn't for him. He liked the independence: "You can't b.s. your way around." He bought his forty-two-foot fishing boat, the Tar Baby, in 1994.

He believes that he's a steward of the state's fisheries as well as someone making his living from them. Hemilright is involved with state and federal fishery boards, helping to monitor the conditions in the state's waters and working to balance the needs of commercial and recreational fishing. He's active in a national program that brings fishermen and farmers into classrooms to teach K-12 kids about where their food come from. Hemilright visits coastal middle schools as well. "I show my log books, talk about water temperature, have a slide show of my gear. I tell about how I make my livelihood," he says.

As it is for most watermen, making a living is becoming more challenging for Hemilright. On the Tar Baby, he points out required monitoring equipment, including an on-deck camera and video screen used during tuna season, which costs fifty dollars a month. Stacks of gear on shore—he works six to seven different fish seasons, each with its own equipment requirements—must be maintained. He faces constantly changing government regulations on when and where he can fish. "It costs more to use local seafood because it costs more to catch it," Hemilright says. "But it's the best, and it's good for you." He adds that people often don't figure freshness into the equation: "If it's caught this day, there's shelf life on it. It will be good in the refrigerator a few days."

For Hemilright, being a fisherman is more than finding the best fish. It's also helping to build demand for the catch and ways for it to reach inland consumers, as well as consumer education and balancing the protection of fishing grounds with the needs of fishermen.

"I believe in what we do. This is your resource as well as mine," he says. "I'm not here to eat the last fish."

Locals Seafood

Mini Hot Crab Tarts

If you love crab dip, you'll love these nibbles. They can be made a day ahead and refrigerated; just heat for ten minutes in a 300° oven. Pie expert Ken Haedrich generously gave permission to include this recipe from his book *Dinner Pies*. If you've never made pie dough, try it; Ken's directions ensure success. The dough, which works for savory or sweet pies, can be made ahead and frozen.

1 recipe Go-To Pie Dough, divided as instructed in the
    first step and refrigerated (recipe follows)

1 tablespoon unsalted butter

½ cup finely chopped white or yellow onion

1 medium clove garlic, minced

½ teaspoon Old Bay or other seafood seasoning

4 ounces cream cheese, at room temperature

¼ cup mayonnaise

3 tablespoons sour cream

1 tablespoon finely chopped pickled jalapeño peppers,
    plus a little of the pickling juice

½ teaspoon Dijon mustard

½ teaspoon Worcestershire sauce

5 ounces drained and flaked canned crabmeat

1 cup grated sharp or extra-sharp cheddar cheese

¼ teaspoon salt

Black pepper, to taste

Prepare the dough, dividing it into 3 equal pieces. Flatten each piece into a ½-inch-thick disk and wrap the disks individually in plastic wrap. Refrigerate for at least 1½ hours. Get out a standard 12-cup muffin pan and a 3- or 3½-inch round biscuit cutter and set them aside.

Working with 1 piece of dough at a time (and leaving the others in the refrigerator), roll it into a thin circle 8½ to 9 inches in diameter on a lightly floured work surface. Keeping the cuts close together, cut the dough into rounds with your biscuit cutter. You should be able to get 4 circles out of each piece of dough. Slide each round down evenly into a muffin cup, pushing it gently so you don't stretch it. The dough should have a nicely defined (not rounded off) crease around the bottom perimeter of the cup. Repeat with the other 2 pieces of dough, lining the rest of the cups. Refrigerate the muffin pan. (Gather your scraps and press together. Wrap well, freeze, and use later to make a small pie.)

While the shells chill, make the filling. Melt the butter in a small skillet over medium heat and add the onions. Sauté gently for 7 to 8 minutes, stirring in the garlic and seafood seasoning right at the end. Remove from the heat and set aside.

Using an electric mixer, gently beat the cream cheese, mayonnaise, and sour cream until smooth. Blend in the chopped jalapeños, 2 to 3 teaspoons of the jalapeño juice, the mustard, and the Worcestershire sauce. Add the onion mixture, scraping the pan well to get out all the seasoning. Using a wooden spoon, stir in the crabmeat, cheddar cheese, and salt, and season with pepper; stir until evenly mixed. Cover and refrigerate for 30 minutes. Meanwhile, preheat the oven to 375°.

Divide the filling among the shells, smoothing the tops. Bake until slightly puffed and golden, 22 to 25 minutes. Transfer the pan to a rack and cool for 10 to 15 minutes. Run a spoon around each tart to loosen, then lift them out, and let them cool a bit more on the rack. These are best served warm and can easily be reheated on a baking sheet in a moderate oven for 10 minutes. Do not microwave.

Go-To Pie Dough

8 tablespoons (1 stick) cold unsalted butter plus 2 tablespoons
    cold vegetable shortening, or 10 tablespoons cold unsalted butter,
    cut into ½-inch cubes
1½ cups all-purpose flour
1½ teaspoons cornstarch
½ teaspoon salt
2 teaspoons white vinegar
Scant ⅓ cup cold water

Put the butter and shortening cubes in a single layer on a flour-dusted plate, with the shortening off to one side of the plate by itself. Refrigerate for at least 30 minutes. Combine the flour, cornstarch, and salt in a bowl and refrigerate that mixture also. Pour the vinegar into a 1-cup glass measure. Add enough cold water to equal ⅓ cup liquid. Refrigerate.

When you're ready to mix the pastry, transfer the flour mixture to a food processor. Pulse several times to mix. Remove the lid and scatter about 6 tablespoons of the butter—a little more than half of the total fat—over the dry mixture. Pulse the machine 5 times—that's 5 one-second pulses—followed by an uninterrupted 5-second run. Remove the lid and add the remaining fat. Give the machine 6 or 7 one-second pulses.

Remove the lid and loosen the mixture with a big fork; you'll have a range of fat clods, most quite small but a few larger ones as well. With the lid off, drizzle about half of the liquid over the mixture. Replace the lid and give the machine 3 very quick, ½-second pulses. Remove the lid, loosen the mixture with your fork, and add the rest of the liquid. Pulse briefly 3 or 4 times, just as before. The mixture will still look crumbly, but the crumbs will be starting to get a little clumpier.

Transfer the contents of your processor to a large bowl, one large enough to get your hands in. Start rubbing the crumbs together, as if you were making a streusel topping—what you're doing is redistributing the butter and moisture without overworking the dough. (Note: If your dough mixture came out of the food processor more clumpy than crumblike, don't worry. Just pack it together like a snowball, knead it very gently 2 or 3 times and proceed to the next step.)

You can accomplish the same thing by "smearing" the crumbs down the sides of the bowl with your fingers. When the dough starts to gather in large clumps, pack it like a snowball and knead gently, 3 or 4 times, on a lightly floured surface.

Put the dough on a long piece of plastic wrap and flatten it into a 1-inch-thick disk. wrap tightly in plastic wrap and refrigerate for at least 1½ to 2 hours, overnight is fine. (You can also slip the wrapped dough into a gallon-size plastic freezer bag and freeze it for up to 2 months. Thaw overnight in the refrigerator before using.)

From *Dinner Pies*, by Ken Haedrich. © 2015 Ken Haedrich. Used by permission of Harvard Common Press.

Atlantic Caviar and Sturgeon, Happy Valley

RAISING CAROLINA CAVIAR

With ridged backs, bony exoskeletons, and no scales, sturgeons look like prehistoric creatures—they're Ice Age survivors. Yet these living dinosaurs are the source for the ultimate luxury food: caviar, which is salted and cured sturgeon roe.

The Atlantic coast had one of the world's largest wild sturgeon populations until the late 1800s, when the sturgeons fell victim to overfishing. Today, overfishing has endangered the Russian wild sturgeon, making some chefs reluctant to use Russian caviar. Atlantic Caviar and Sturgeon believes that farming may be the answer for caviar, and the fish tastes good, too.

Entrepreneurs Bill White and Joe Doll came up with the idea in 1998, found the land about ninety miles west of Charlotte, and started raising fish in 2005. Sturgeon grow very slowly, taking at least five years before reaching harvest weight, so it was 2012 before the first caviar was harvested. By then, White had died. He left his part of the business to North Carolina State University, which is now involved in research and other aspects of the project.

The farm raises Russian sturgeon, which grow in the tanks to a manageable two to three feet long. The tanks use well water, which is filtered and oxygenated in a recirculating system, then mixed with 15 percent freshwater and returned to the tanks. Water that's removed is placed in a holding pond and used on nearby farms. Waste is composted for fertilizer.

At the moment, the only way to tell whether a sturgeon is female is to do an ultrasound, but researchers are trying to develop a simpler blood test to determine gender.

The sturgeon is dispatched with a mallet blow to the head. The egg sac, which can contain up to four pounds of roe, is opened and rinsed. The eggs are salted, then packed in weighted containers, and placed in a cooler. The weights press out excess liquid and salt. After twenty-four hours the weights are removed, and the caviar is then aged for two to three months.

The firm, mild-tasting sturgeon meat is tasty, too. It's popular smoked, and the company has sold meat to a New York smokehouse.

For more information, visit atlanticcaviar andsturgeon.com.

Monica's Curried Fried Shrimp

My friend Monica Bhide writes compellingly about food and her Indian heritage in her cookbooks such as *Modern Spice* and her novel, *Karma and the Art of Butter Chicken*. Monica says this appetizer is a favorite of her family in Washington, D.C. With the growing number of Indian immigrants to North Carolina, the ingredients are easy to find here. Adapt the recipe to your family's preferences by using mild, medium, or hot curry powder.

Makes 4 to 6 servings

1 pound large shrimp, peeled, deveined, and tails removed

2 tablespoons curry powder

4 tablespoons grated fresh ginger

4 tablespoons fresh lemon juice

Salt, to taste

2 eggs

4 heaping tablespoons all-purpose flour

4 cups vegetable oil

Chutney (such as Major Grey) for serving

Prepare the shrimp by cutting along the back of the shrimp without slicing all the way through, then spread the meat out like a butterfly.

In a shallow bowl, combine the curry powder, ginger, lemon juice, and salt. Mix well. In a second bowl, beat the eggs. Place the flour in another shallow bowl.

Coat each shrimp with the spice mixture, brushing off any clumps that form. Dredge the shrimp lightly in flour, then dip them in the egg, allowing any excess egg to drip off. Coat again lightly with flour. Place the coated shrimp on a platter.

In a deep fryer or deep Dutch oven, heat the oil over medium-high heat until hot but not smoking. Then lower the heat to medium and, working in batches, place a few of the shrimp in the pan and deep-fry until golden brown. Do not overload the oil. (See frying tips in "Best Basics," page 16.) Remove the shrimp with a slotted spoon and set on paper towels to drain. Serve warm with chutney.

Dean Neff's Baked Oysters with Shrimp

Makes about
10 oysters

Seasons of the Sea dinners at Piedmont Restaurant in Durham high-lighted the seasonality of seafood, along with the talents of Piedmont's chef John May and guest chefs. This appetizer from chef Dean Neff of Pinpoint in Wilmington is a different way to do baked oysters, and he kindly shared the recipe. It's easy to double, too. Be sure to scrub the oysters thoroughly under cold running water to remove dirt clinging to the outside, and keep them cold until you need them.

¼ pound medium shrimp, peeled and deveined,
    shells reserved
¼ cup canola oil
1 scant tablespoon palm oil (see Notes)
1½ teaspoons unsalted butter
2 tablespoons minced yellow onion
1 medium clove garlic, thinly shaved
⅛ teaspoon crushed dried red pepper
⅛ teaspoon smoked paprika
1½ teaspoons all-purpose flour
1½ teaspoons cream
2 tablespoons whole milk
1½ teaspoons fresh lemon juice
Salt, to taste
¼ teaspoon minced fresh thyme
¼ teaspoon chopped fresh oregano
10 fresh oysters in the shell
Panko
Lemon wedges

Thinly slice the shrimp and set aside.

Put the canola oil in a small saucepan over medium-high heat. Add the shrimp shells and fry, stirring, until very golden and crispy, 5 to 6 minutes. Remove the shells and drain well on paper towels, patting gently to remove excess oil. Place the shells and palm oil in a small food processor or blender. Process until the mixture is very smooth, scraping the sides of the bowl occasionally. Set aside.

Put the butter in a small saucepan over low heat. When the butter is melted, add the minced onions, garlic, red pepper, and paprika.

Sauté until soft but not brown. Add the flour and stir well to blend completely. Cook, stirring, over low heat for 3 minutes. Add the cream, milk, shrimp, and lemon juice, and raise the heat to medium-low. Cook, stirring, until the shrimp are cooked through, 3 to 4 minutes. Season with salt to taste, then add the fresh herbs. Set aside.

Preheat the oven to 375°. Open the oysters (see Notes). Make sure they're free of bits of shell, and use the oyster knife to detach the muscle holding the oyster to the bottom shell. Leave the oyster in the shell half and discard the other half shell. Divide the shrimp mixture evenly over the oysters. Sprinkle each oyster lightly with panko, then top with the palm oil mixture.

Place the oysters in a baking pan. Bake until the oysters are hot throughout and the bread crumbs are golden brown, 5 to 10 minutes. Serve warm with lemon wedges to squeeze on top.

NOTES: Dean uses sustainably sourced palm oil. Palm oil from unsustainable sources has been linked to rain forest destruction and human rights abuses. You could substitute coconut oil, but it would have a stronger flavor.

If you find it difficult to open the oysters, either use the approach described in "Best Basics," page 13, or lightly steam them: place them in a steamer basket in a pot containing a few inches of boiling water and steam, covered, for 2 to 3 minutes, just until they barely begin to open. Lightly cooking the oysters first doesn't affect the final result, but the baking time will be shorter.

Shrimp Dumplings with Linda

When my Raleigh friend Linda Miller lived in Japan, she soaked up the culture and food, including learning to make dumplings. We often meet "to dumple," turning out batches of delicious bites and conversation. My dumplings aren't as beautifully pleated as hers, but they still taste great, so don't worry if yours aren't perfect. Linda says that in Japan, making dumplings is a group activity, so invite friends and turn it into a party. Purchase bottled dumpling sauce and gyoza wrappers at Asian markets or large supermarkets.

Makes about 44 dumplings

1½ cups chopped bok choy

1 small knob fresh ginger, peeled

1 small clove garlic, peeled

1½ cups chopped Chinese chives (*nira*) or green onion

2 pounds shrimp, shelled and deveined

1 tablespoon potato starch or cornstarch

1 egg, beaten

1 tablespoon sesame oil

1 tablespoon soy sauce

1 tablespoon sake (optional)

2 (12-ounce) packages round gyoza wrappers

1 to 2 tablespoons vegetable oil

Dumpling sauce for serving

Coarsely chop the bok choy, ginger, and garlic in a food processor but do not purée. Place in a strainer or a bowl lined with paper towels to absorb excess moisture. Chop the Chinese chives or green onions and place in a strainer or bowl lined with paper towels. Make sure the shrimp is as dry as possible, then coarsely chop in the food processor.

In a large bowl, combine the bok choy, ginger, garlic, Chinese chives or green onions, and shrimp. Add the potato starch or cornstarch, egg, sesame oil, and soy sauce, plus sake, if using. Stir to combine.

To make the dumplings, place a gyoza wrapper on a work surface. Dip your finger in water and moisten the edge. Place a scant teaspoon of filling in the center of the wrapper. Don't overfill or the dumplings may pop open in cooking. Fold the wrapper over the filling and press the left side of the edge together. Pleat the edge together 5 or 6 times to seal. Repeat with the remaining wrappers and filling.

Heat about 1 tablespoon oil in a nonstick frying pan over medium-high heat. Place the dumplings close together in the pan; it's OK if they touch. Fry for a couple of minutes until they begin to brown on the bottom. Add 2 or 3 tablespoons of water, enough to cover the bottom of the pan, then cover and reduce the heat to medium. Let the dumplings steam for 3 to 5 minutes, adding a little more water if the pan becomes dry. The dumplings will be done when they begin to look translucent and moist and you smell the fragrance of cooked shrimp.

Serve immediately with dumpling sauce.

NOTE: The dumplings can be frozen before cooking. Place them on a tray in the freezer, then transfer to freezer bags after they harden.

Shrimp Avocado Toast

Combining rich avocado and sweet shrimp makes a quick appetizer that's great as a party snack, or serve it with a salad for lunch. The number of servings depends on the size of the bread slices. Be sure to use good-quality fresh bread and juicy tomatoes. Crabmeat could be substituted for the shrimp.

Makes 8 servings

8 slices good-quality bread

2 cups chopped cherry tomatoes

4 tablespoons chopped green onion

24 medium shrimp, cooked, peeled, and thinly sliced

About 2 teaspoons olive oil

Salt and black pepper, to taste

1 large, ripe avocado, peeled and pitted

Lime wedges

Capers for garnish

Lightly toast the bread slices.

In a small bowl, combine the chopped cherry tomatoes, green onions, and shrimp. Stir in enough olive oil to moisten the mixture and season with salt and pepper.

Mash the avocado meat in a small bowl. Smear a thin layer of avocado on each bread slice and sprinkle lightly with salt. Top with the tomato-shrimp mixture. Squeeze lime juice over the slices, sprinkle with pepper, and top with capers. Serve immediately with additional lime wedges.

Judith's Hickory Planked Shrimp with Bearnaise Butter

Makes 4 to 6
servings

Where there's smoke, there's often Judith Fertig, who with Karen Adler are the BBQ Queens. As the authors of several books on grilling and smoking, they know their fire. Judith shared this recipe that combines shrimp and the aroma of hickory. Find hickory or cedar grilling planks and hickory chips at hardware stores, and be sure to soak them thoroughly before using. Shellfish cooks fast, so for a smoky flavor, get the hickory chips going first.

1 cup (2 sticks) unsalted butter, softened

¼ cup chopped shallot

¼ cup chopped fresh tarragon

2 tablespoons white wine vinegar

1 teaspoon hot pepper sauce (such as Tabasco or Texas Pete), or to taste

2 pounds extra-large shrimp, shelled and deveined

Loaf of crusty French or Italian bread

Soak 2 hickory or cedar grilling planks in water for at least 1 hour.

Prepare the Bearnaise Butter: Combine the butter, shallots, tarragon, vinegar, and hot pepper sauce in a small bowl and stir with a fork until well blended. Spoon into a clean bowl, cover, and leave at room temperature for 1 hour for the flavors to blend.

Prepare an indirect fire in your grill, with a hot fire on one side and no fire on the other. For a charcoal fire, when the coals have ashed over, sprinkle a handful of fine hickory wood chips on the coals. For a gas grill, place the wood chips in a smoker box or make a packet out of aluminum foil with holes punched in the top; place the smoker box or packet over direct heat in the back of the grill.

Divide the shrimp between the 2 planks and dollop with 4 tablespoons of the Bearnaise Butter. When you can see the first wisps of smoke, place the planks on the no-heat side of the grill. As the butter melts, toss the shrimp in it to coat. Close the grill lid and let the shrimp plank-cook for 15 to 20 minutes or until they are pink, opaque, and just firm.

Serve immediately from the planks with bread and the remaining Bearnaise Butter.

Soups and Salads

»»

Ricky Moore's Chowan County Shellfish "Muddle"

ALTERNATIVES:
flounder, rockfish,
triggerfish

Makes 4 to 6
servings

Durham chef Ricky Moore grew up in eastern North Carolina and has cooked all over the world. His heart's desire was to open a fish shack, so he started Saltbox Seafood Joint, where he prepares the freshest North Carolina seafood, plus all the sides, from scratch. I tasted this dish at one of Piedmont Restaurant in Durham's Seasons of the Sea dinners where Ricky was guest chef, and he shared his recipe. You'll never suspect that there's no butter or cream in the rich purée that forms the base of his version of a traditional muddle.

2 tablespoons extra-virgin olive oil, plus more for cooking the fish
2 teaspoons chopped garlic
2 cups chopped leeks (white parts only, from 2 or 3 leeks)
¼ teaspoon salt
1 large head cauliflower, chopped
7 cups clam, chicken, or vegetable broth
¼ cup coarsely chopped raw, unsalted cashews
2 pounds monkfish fillets, cut into 4 to 6 serving pieces
Salt, black pepper, and Tabasco to taste
Meat from 12 to 18 steamed clams (for steaming instructions,
    see "Best Basics," page 15)
12 medium shrimp, cooked, peeled, deveined, and tails removed
3 tablespoons chopped fresh chives for garnish

In a large saucepan, heat the oil over medium heat and sauté the garlic, leeks, and ¼ teaspoon of salt for about 3 minutes, until the vegetables are soft. Add the cauliflower and sauté for another minute.

Add the broth, then increase the heat to high and bring just to a boil. Reduce the heat to medium and simmer for 20 to 30 minutes, until the cauliflower is completely tender. Remove the saucepan from the heat and allow the mixture to cool slightly, then stir in the cashews.

Pour the mixture into a blender and purée on high for about 1 minute, until smooth and creamy. You will need to do this in batches.

Return the mixture to the saucepan and keep it warm over low heat. Season with salt, pepper, and Tabasco to taste.

Heat a large sauté pan over medium-high heat and add enough olive oil to cover the bottom. Season the fish with salt and pepper, then pan-sear on both sides until cooked through.

To serve, ladle the cauliflower mixture into warm bowls and place the pan-seared fish portion on top, then evenly distribute the clams and shrimp. Sprinkle with chives and serve.

Eastern North Carolina Fish Stew in the Slow Cooker

ALTERNATIVES:
drum, mahi,
dogfish,
sheepshead

Makes 6 servings

Fish stew that includes poached eggs is an eastern North Carolina tradition, which cooks concoct from old recipe cards or simply from memory. After preparing it the usual way, by simmering on the stove, I thought it might work well in a slow cooker—and it did, with a few adjustments. Add the fish near the end of the cooking time to prevent overcooking. I poached the eggs separately, but if your slow cooker has a simmer function, you could try poaching the eggs in the broth, as is traditional.

1½ pounds potatoes, peeled and cut into ¼-inch slices

1 large white or yellow onion, thinly sliced

4 medium cloves garlic, sliced

1½ teaspoons salt

¼ teaspoon crushed dried red pepper

2 tablespoons tomato paste

4 slices bacon

1½ pounds monkfish fillets, cut into 6 pieces

6 eggs

Lightly spray the bottom of the slow cooker with nonstick cooking spray. Layer half of the potatoes, then half of the onions, half of the garlic, half of the salt, and half of the red pepper. Repeat the layers with the remaining vegetables and seasonings.

Whisk the tomato paste into 2 cups of warm water until it dissolves, then pour over the layers. Add enough water to cover the layers, about 8 cups. Cover and cook on High for 3 hours.

Fry the bacon until crispy, drain, and crumble. Reserve the bacon grease.

After 3 hours, pour 1 tablespoon of warm bacon grease into the stew, then nestle the fish gently into the liquid until completely covered. Cover and cook for 30 minutes to 1 hour or until the fish is flaky and cooked through. Thicker fillets will take more time than thinner fillets.

Poach the eggs in a pot of simmering water.

To serve, ladle the stew into bowls, including 1 piece of fish per serving, then add 1 poached egg. Top with crumbled bacon.

Grilled Monkfish Salad with Norma's Ginger-Citrus Dressing

ALTERNATIVES:
snapper, sea bass, shrimp

Makes 4 to 5 servings

I got excited about dressing—yes, salad dressing—when my friend Norma DeCamp Burns brought a salad to a potluck. It was so flavorful and I knew it would go well with smoky grilled fish. She was very kind to share her recipe. I changed one of the ingredients because it's hard to find: calamondin, a tropical citrus fruit that she grows in a greenhouse. Tangelo is a great substitute.

FOR THE DRESSING

½ of a medium tangelo or 1 small tangerine

½ cup white balsamic vinegar

¼ cup apple cider vinegar

1 large clove garlic

½ cup chopped green onion, green part only

Juice of 1 Meyer lemon (see Note)

1 teaspoon peeled and chopped fresh ginger

½ cup peeled and chopped fresh pear

3 tablespoons Seville orange marmalade or ginger preserves

2 tablespoons honey

½ cup olive oil

½ teaspoon salt

FOR THE SALAD

Olive oil

10 asparagus spears

3 baby leeks, separated and rinsed well

3 small or 2 large bunches romaine, kept as whole as possible

1 medium tomato, cut into about 8 thin wedges

1 pound monkfish fillets

Salt and black pepper, to taste

½ large, medium-firm avocado, peeled, pitted, and thinly sliced

For the dressing, cut the tangelo or tangerine into small pieces and remove any seeds; do not peel. Place in a blender. Add the vinegars, garlic, green onions, Meyer lemon juice, ginger, pear, and preserves. Blend or pulse a few times to combine. Add the honey, olive oil, and salt. Blend until pourable. The dressing can be made ahead and refrigerated for up to 2 days.

For the salad, prepare a charcoal or gas grill for direct cooking and place an oiled grill tray over the grate.

Toss the asparagus and leeks lightly with olive oil. Place on the grill tray. Cook, turning frequently with tongs, until slightly charred. Remove the vegetables to a platter. Lightly toss the romaine in olive oil and grill, turning frequently, until slightly wilted and charred on all sides. This will take only a couple of minutes, depending on the size of the bunches. Watch carefully to prevent burning and turn often. Remove the grilled romaine to the platter. Place the tomato wedges on the grill tray and cook, turning with a spatula, until slightly charred and wilted on both sides; this will take only 1 or 2 minutes. Add them to the platter with the other vegetables.

Lightly coat the monkfish with oil, and season with salt and pepper. Grill, turning once, until cooked through. Cut the fish into 1-inch slices.

Arrange the platter with the tomatoes and fish on top of the other vegetables. Place the sliced avocado on top. Drizzle 1 to 2 tablespoons of Norma's Ginger-Citrus Dressing over the salad, or to taste. Serve immediately.

NOTE: If you can't find Meyer lemons, use regular lemon juice, then taste the dressing at the end and add honey, if necessary.

The Asbury's Warm Kale Salad with Mountain Trout

Makes 4 servings
as a side salad; 2 as
a main dish salad.

Chef Matthew Krenz, culinary director and executive chef at The Asbury in Charlotte's Dunhill Hotel, says this hearty salad is one of his most popular items. Matthew smokes his own trout, but purchasing smoked trout makes the recipe quick to prepare. (If you'd like to smoke your own, see "Best Basics," page 19.) Pass extra dressing around in case people want more or save it for other uses—my tester found it addictive. Look for green brine-packed peppercorns near the capers in the grocery store—but they're not capers, so don't confuse the two.

FOR THE DRESSING

½ cup mayonnaise (see Note)

½ cup crème fraîche

½ cup grated Parmesan cheese

1 tablespoon fresh lemon juice

1½ tablespoons green brine-packed peppercorns,
    drained and roughly chopped

2 medium cloves garlic, chopped

Salt and black pepper, to taste

FOR THE CROUTONS

3 tablespoons unsalted butter

1 to 3 medium whole cloves garlic, peeled

2 cups large bread cubes

Salt and black pepper, to taste

2 to 3 dashes of paprika

FOR THE SALAD

About 3 tablespoons canola oil

8 to 10 cups chopped Tuscan or curly kale

2 tablespoons white wine

1 tablespoon chopped shallot

1 tablespoon chopped garlic

Salt and black pepper, to taste

4 to 5 ounces smoked trout, cut into chunks

2 tablespoons pine nuts, toasted

3 tablespoons grated Asiago cheese

For the dressing, combine all the ingredients until creamy and smooth. The dressing can be made several days ahead and refrigerated.

For the croutons, melt the butter in a large sauté pan over medium heat and add the garlic. Sauté until the garlic becomes fragrant but not brown, then add the bread cubes. Sauté until the bread is well coated with the butter. Remove the garlic cloves. Lightly salt and pepper the croutons, sprinkle with paprika, and toss to combine.

Preheat the oven to 350°. Spread the croutons on a baking sheet and bake for 12 minutes or until golden brown and crispy. Let cool completely. The croutons can be made a few days ahead and stored in an airtight container.

For the salad, heat a wok or a saucepan large enough to hold the kale over high heat. Add enough canola oil to coat the pan. Add the kale and let it sit for 45 seconds or until you see some charring on the bottom leaves. Then add the white wine, shallots, garlic, salt, and pepper. Cook, stirring, until the kale is tender but still bright green.

Transfer the kale mixture to a large mixing bowl. Add the trout and just enough dressing to coat the salad. Toss until the ingredients are evenly coated. Add the pine nuts and croutons, then sprinkle the cheese on top. Serve while still warm. Alternatively, you can let diners add the amount of croutons they want to their individual servings instead of mixing them in.

NOTE: The chef uses house-made aioli in the dressing but says mayo is a fine substitute.

Grilled Mackerel Potato Salad

ALTERNATIVES:
tuna, trout, catfish

Makes 6 servings

As either a light lunch or a hearty side, this recipe will please both fish fans and potato salad lovers. The idea is based on the classic French salade niçoise. Smoked trout would work well in this dish, too.

½ pound mackerel fillets

2 pounds small new potatoes

¼ pound green beans

¼ cup chopped red onion

2 tablespoons chopped black olives

2 hard-cooked eggs, coarsely chopped

¾ cup olive oil, plus more for the mackerel

3 tablespoons sherry vinegar

½ teaspoon chopped garlic

2 teaspoons Dijon mustard

¾ teaspoon salt

¾ teaspoon black pepper

½ cup chopped fresh Italian parsley

Rub the fish liberally with olive oil. Grill over direct heat on a gas or charcoal grill, or use an oiled stovetop grill pan, turning once, until cooked through. Set aside until cool enough to touch, then flake into small pieces.

Place the potatoes in a large pot and add enough water to cover. Bring to a boil, then cook at a rolling boil until the potatoes can be pierced easily with a sharp knife, 15 to 20 minutes. Drain and let the potatoes cool until you can handle them, then cut them into chunks of similar size.

Break the green beans into approximately 1-inch pieces, then steam over boiling water or in the microwave until cooked but still bright green. Place the green beans and potatoes in a large bowl. Add the red onions, olives, eggs, and fish. Toss to combine.

In a small bowl, whisk together the ¾ cup olive oil, vinegar, garlic, mustard, salt, and pepper. Pour the dressing over the salad and toss.

The salad can be served immediately, but the flavor improves if it's covered and refrigerated for a few hours or even overnight. Sprinkle on the parsley just before serving.

Elliott's Italian Soup with Flounder

My friend Elliott Warnock in Chapel Hill is a man of many talents, including cooking. He found this soup recipe in a 1930s collection of southern Italian recipes and has made changes over the years, turning it into a family favorite. "It has a deep flavor despite its simplicity," he says. Elliott advises folding in the fish gently so that it won't fall apart (although the soup is still good if it does). Serve with crusty bread.

ALTERNATIVES:
perch, striped
bass, triggerfish

Makes 6 servings

2 tablespoons olive oil

1 tablespoon unsalted butter

1 shallot, minced

1 cup finely chopped white or yellow onion

½ cup chopped carrot

1 medium clove garlic, minced

¼ cup chopped celery

1 teaspoon anchovy paste

6 to 7 plum tomatoes, peeled and chopped, or

    1 (14½ ounce) can diced tomatoes, with liquid

1 (15-ounce) can tomato sauce

½ cup dry white wine

1 to 2 bay leaves

Salt and black pepper, to taste

¼ cup chopped green onion

2 to 3 pounds skinless flounder fillets, cut into 2- to 3-inch pieces.

¼ cup chopped fresh parsley

Place the oil and butter in a Dutch oven over medium-high heat. Add shallots and cook, stirring, for 30 seconds, then add the onions and carrots. Cook, stirring, until the onions begin to soften. Stir in the garlic, celery, and anchovy paste. Cook, stirring, until the aroma of the garlic rises, but don't let it brown.

Add the tomatoes, tomato sauce, wine, bay leaf, and 1 cup water. Simmer on medium to medium-high heat for 10 minutes, uncovered. Season with salt and pepper, cover, and reduce the heat to a low simmer. Simmer for 15 minutes.

Stir the soup, then add the green onions. Place the fish in the sauce gently. Cover and simmer for 5 minutes or until the fish is cooked through. Top with parsley and serve.

Amanda's New England Clam Chowder

Makes 6 to 8
servings

Amanda Cushman's rich chowder is loaded with fresh clams. The Chapel Hill culinary instructor and food writer has contributed to numerous magazines and served as a private chef. Find out more about her here: www.chapelhillcookingclasses.com.

4 slices thick bacon, diced

1 tablespoon vegetable oil

1 medium white or yellow onion, diced

3 stalks celery, diced

2 medium cloves garlic, minced

2 bay leaves

2 teaspoons chopped fresh thyme, plus 2 sprigs, divided

3 cups fish stock (see Note)

2 medium baking potatoes, peeled and diced

Salt and black pepper, to taste

1¼ cups whole milk

1½ cups white wine

4 pounds littleneck clams, rinsed well

1 tablespoon unsalted butter

5 tablespoons all-purpose flour

½ cup heavy cream

2 tablespoons finely chopped fresh parsley

In a medium skillet, cook the bacon until crisp, about 6 minutes. Drain the bacon on a paper towel.

Heat the oil in a medium-size wide saucepan over medium-high heat. Sauté the onions, celery, garlic, bay leaves, and chopped thyme until the onions are golden, about 7 minutes. Deglaze the pan by adding 1 cup of the fish stock and stir, scraping up all the brown bits on the bottom of the pan as the stock simmers. Add the remaining stock, plus potatoes, salt, and pepper. Reduce the heat to medium-low and simmer until the potatoes are tender, about 15 minutes. Add the milk and bring to a simmer, but don't allow it to boil.

Meanwhile, bring the wine to a boil in a medium saucepan. Add the clams, thyme sprigs, and butter, and season with salt and pepper. Cover and simmer for 5 to 8 minutes, lifting the lid occasionally and removing clams as they open. Reserve the cooking liquid. When the clams are cool enough to handle, remove the meat from the shells. Discard the shells and reserve the meat. Strain the cooking liquid to remove grit and add it to the soup.

Whisk together the flour and cream in a small bowl. Add to the soup by spoonfuls, whisking after each addition, until the soup thickens. Taste and add salt if needed.

Add the clam meat to the soup and remove the soup from the heat. Serve the chowder in large bowls and garnish with parsley.

NOTE: Look for fish stock in the freezer sections of larger supermarkets or at your fishmonger's. If you can't find it, use bottled clam juice instead.

Hatteras-Style Clam Chowder

I visit Hatteras Island on the state's beautiful Outer Banks each year. Clam chowder there is a milk-free, broth-based version. I've heard from historians that this may be because it was difficult to raise cows on the rugged island, which for generations was accessible only by boat. Use plenty of clams—you can't have too many.

Makes 6 to 8 servings

55 littleneck clams, rinsed well

3 slices bacon, chopped

1 cup chopped white or yellow onion

½ cup chopped celery

2 cups peeled and chopped potatoes

Salt

1 teaspoon fresh thyme

Chopped celery leaves or parsley for serving

Steam the clams (see "Best Basics," page 15). Remove the clam meat from the shells and reserve. Drain the cooking broth through a strainer lined with cheesecloth and reserve.

In a large Dutch oven or soup pot over medium heat, fry the bacon until crispy and drain on paper towels. Leave about 2 tablespoons of bacon fat in the pot (spoon out any extra) and warm over medium heat. Cook the onions and celery, stirring, until soft but not brown, 3 to 4 minutes.

Add the reserved clam cooking liquid plus enough water to total 6 cups. Add the potatoes and a generous sprinkling of salt. Bring the mixture to a boil, then reduce the heat, cover, and simmer until the potatoes are tender but not mushy, 20 to 30 minutes.

When the potatoes are tender, turn off the heat, then stir in the clams and thyme. Don't cook the clams further or they may become rubbery. Taste, and add salt if needed.

To serve, garnish each bowl of chowder with cooked bacon and celery leaves or parsley.

Gumbo with Greens and Oysters

Makes 6 to 8
servings

"Did you put collards in this?" asked my collard-hating husband when he tasted this gumbo. I didn't, but I could have, and so could you. (Use the small-leafed cabbage collards, which are more tender than the large ones.) Give your full attention to making the roux—no texting, calling, or Instagramming.

1 pint shucked oysters with their liquor

½ cup vegetable oil

½ cup all-purpose flour

1 cup chopped white or yellow onion

1 cup chopped green bell pepper

1 cup chopped celery

2 medium cloves garlic, chopped

1 bay leaf

½ teaspoon Aleppo pepper, or ¼ teaspoon crushed
   dried red pepper

¼ teaspoon smoked paprika (optional)

½ teaspoon salt

6 cups chopped fresh greens (spinach, collards, kale,
   chard, or a combination)

Your preferred kind of cooked rice for serving

Drain the oysters and reserve their liquor. Cover the oysters and refrigerate.

Make a roux: Heat the oil in a large, heavy-bottomed pot on medium high and add the flour. Cook, whisking continuously, until the roux is a dark golden brown. Adjust the heat or slide the pot off the heat if the roux begins to cook too quickly. Do not stop whisking or the roux may burn.

When the roux is dark enough, add the onions, bell peppers, celery, and garlic. Lower the heat to medium and cook, stirring with a spoon, until the vegetables are soft, 3 to 4 minutes.

Stir in the bay leaf, Aleppo or red pepper, paprika (if using), salt, 8 cups of water, and liquor from the oysters. Stir in the chopped greens. Reduce the heat to low, cover, and simmer for 45 minutes or until the greens are meltingly tender.

Stir in the oysters. Raise the heat if necessary to return the gumbo to a simmer. Simmer, covered, until the oysters begin to curl on the edges, 6 minutes or so, depending on the oysters' size. Taste and add salt if needed. Serve in bowls over rice.

Chilled Cucumber Seafood Soup

Makes 6 servings

I was proud to harvest the first two cucumbers from my backyard garden, which I grew in discarded rectangular recycling bins. They went into this summer soup along with shrimp. For a richer soup, use whole milk or buttermilk, but I like the light flavor of almond milk in this soup—and dairy-allergic diners can enjoy it.

2 large cucumbers, peeled and seeded

6 to 8 large yellow cherry tomatoes, halved

2 cups almond milk

1 teaspoon salt, or to taste

2 tablespoons chopped fresh chives, plus more for garnish

½ pound small shrimp, cooked and peeled

Roughly chop the cucumbers and place them in the work bowl of a food processor. Pulse several times to create a coarse paste. Add the cherry tomatoes and pulse a few more times. Add the almond milk, salt, and 2 tablespoons of the chives, and process until the mixture is smooth.

Pour the mixture into a large bowl. Stir in the shrimp. Chill the soup for at least 4 hours before serving. Garnish each bowl with additional chopped chives.

Mixed Seafood Bisque

My first experience with fish soups was on a family vacation to the beach, where my father and I sampled a creamy crab soup. We remembered the rich flavor for years. Shrimp and fish join crab in this recipe, which I adapted from one in a Hatteras Volunteer Fire Department Ladies Auxiliary cookbook. Be sure to remove any stray bones from the fish.

Makes 4 to 5 servings

1½ cups chicken broth

1 large potato, peeled and diced

1 small white or yellow onion, finely chopped

½ pound skinless monkfish, black drum, or grouper fillets, cut into small pieces

½ pound medium shrimp, peeled and deveined

¼ cup unsalted butter

¼ cup all-purpose flour

2 cups half-and-half or whole milk, depending on desired richness

1 tablespoon dry sherry

¼ teaspoon Worcestershire sauce

2 to 3 dashes hot pepper sauce (such as Tabasco or Texas Pete), or to taste

Salt and black pepper, to taste

½ pound lump crabmeat

In a large pot, bring the chicken broth and 3 cups of water to a boil. Add the potatoes, onions, fish, and shrimp. Reduce the heat to a high simmer and cook for 3 to 4 minutes, until the vegetables are just tender and the seafood is barely cooked. Set aside.

Make a roux: In a heavy saucepan over medium heat, melt the butter and add the flour. Cook, stirring constantly with a whisk, until the mixture is golden brown. Do not stop stirring or the roux may burn. Reduce the heat to low, and very gradually whisk in the half-and-half or whole milk, stirring constantly, until smooth and thick.

Stir the potato-seafood mixture, including the cooking liquid, into the milk mixture and raise the heat to medium. Stir in the sherry, Worcestershire sauce, hot pepper sauce, salt, pepper, and crabmeat. Simmer gently, stirring, until the bisque is smooth and heated through. Keep warm over low heat if not serving immediately.

Salty Catch's Shrimp Salad

Makes 6 to 8
servings

Size doesn't matter here—get the best fresh shrimp you can find. If you like a creamy salad, use more mayonnaise; for a chunky salad, use less. Thanks to Renee Perry of Salty Catch Seafood Company in Beaufort for providing this recipe for warm-weather salad.

3 pounds shrimp, peeled and deveined
2 hard-cooked eggs, chopped
1 medium green bell pepper, finely chopped
1 medium white or yellow onion, finely chopped
¾ cup finely chopped celery
1 teaspoon celery seed
1 teaspoon fresh lemon juice
½ to ¾ cup mayonnaise
Hot pepper sauce (such as Tabasco or Texas Pete), to taste
Salt and black pepper, to taste

Bring 2 quarts of salted water to a boil in a large pot. Add the shrimp and cook 4 to 6 minutes or until done. Drain and cool down.

When the shrimp are cool enough to handle, cut them into smaller pieces—3 to 5 pieces per shrimp, depending on their size. Place the shrimp in a large bowl. Add the eggs, bell peppers, onions, celery, celery seed, lemon juice, mayonnaise, and a few drops of hot pepper sauce, and mix well. Taste, then season with salt and pepper. Cover and refrigerate 3 to 4 hours or until well chilled before serving.

Locals Seafood, Salty Catch, Walking Fish

GETTING THE CATCH TO THE PEOPLE

At one time, North Carolinians found it difficult to purchase seafood from their very own waters. That's changing, thanks to businesses and groups that are working directly with fishermen, educating the public to increase demand, and building supply routes to the state's markets and restaurants.

Lin Peterson and Ryan Speckman started Locals Seafood in 2010 with a cooler of shrimp in the back of a pickup truck. The goal was to provide the freshest seafood possible and guarantee that it comes from North Carolina fishermen, so they formed direct connections with fishermen and producers. They sell what was caught that day, driving directly to the coast to get it—and can tell you the names of those who caught or raised the fish and shellfish. They also forged commercial connections, and now some of the Triangle's top chefs use seafood from Locals.

Locals sells to the public at Triangle-area farmers' markets and also operates a CSF: community supported fishery. A CSF works like a farm CSA (community supported agriculture), where you pay at the start of the season and then receive produce harvested each week. Visit Locals' market and oyster bar in downtown Raleigh.

Steven Goodwin of Salty Catch Seafood in Beaufort was raised in a fishing family on Cedar Island. "When I was growing up, I would go to the fish house and ask where all the fish was going. Everything was going out of the state," he says. "My dream was to get it going into the state."

Goodwin and Renee Perry started Salty Catch in 2015, delivering to the Triangle area, plus parts of Chatham County. They offer Goodwin's catch plus seafood from other Carteret County fishermen they know. Salty Catch doesn't have markets. Chefs or individuals can contact Perry, find out what's available, and place an order for delivery.

The aptly named Walking Fish was one of the state's first CSFs, started by a group of graduate students at Duke University's Nicholas School of the Environment in 2009. Based in Beaufort with pickup sites in Raleigh and Durham, it has been managed by a fishermen's cooperative since 2011.

In addition to selling local seafood, Walking Fish seeks to reconnect communities and consumers with their food systems and encourage sustainable seafood.

For more information on these fish suppliers, visit their websites:

Locals Seafood: localsseafood.com
Salty Catch: saltycatchseafood.com
Walking Fish: walking-fish.org

Shrimp and Couscous Salad

This do-ahead recipe easily feeds a crowd, and you can stash it in a cooler for a picnic or football tailgate. The tanginess of the lemon juice and artichoke hearts is perfect with the sweet shrimp.

1 (10-ounce) box plain instant couscous

1½ pounds medium shrimp

2 lemon slices, plus 3 to 4 tablespoons fresh lemon juice, divided

1 green bell pepper, chopped

1 red bell pepper, chopped

4 green onions, chopped

1 (12-ounce) jar marinated artichoke hearts, drained and chopped

1¼ cups plain yogurt

¼ cup mayonnaise

Salt and black pepper, to taste

½ cup chopped fresh Italian parsley

Cook the couscous according to package directions. Place it in a large bowl and let it cool to room temperature.

While the couscous is cooling, peel the shrimp. Place the lemon slices in a large saucepan with enough water to cover the shrimp and bring the water to a boil. Add the shrimp and cook for 1 to 2 minutes or until the shrimp turn pink and are done. Drain and let the shrimp cool. Discard the lemon slices.

Stir the green and red bell peppers, green onions, and chopped artichoke hearts into the cooled couscous. In a small bowl, combine the yogurt and mayonnaise. Add enough lemon juice to give the dressing a pourable, but not too thin, consistency. Season with salt and pepper.

Stir the cooled shrimp and the parsley into the couscous mixture. Add the dressing and toss to mix thoroughly. Cover and refrigerate for at least 4 hours or as long as overnight before serving.

A BEVY OF BROTHS

Many people save the bones from roasted chicken to make chicken stock. You can do the same thing with shrimp and fish, and it's just as easy. Shells and heads from raw or cooked shrimp will work for a shrimp stock. Collect them in a bag in the freezer until you have enough. Save the bones and head after cooking a whole fish to make a fish broth, or start with the raw heads and bones and rinse them well. You can freeze shrimp and fish stocks, and they'll be ready for you to use in place of water in all kinds of seafood recipes. Dashi is a classic Japanese stock that can be a base for seafood noodle soups, miso soup, and other dishes. Look for the ingredients in Asian markets.

Shrimp Stock

Shells from a couple pounds of shrimp (cooked or uncooked)
1 medium white or yellow onion, chopped
2 stalks celery (with leaves, if possible), chopped
1 carrot, chopped
3 to 4 whole peppercorns

Place all the ingredients in a large stockpot and add enough water to cover them well. Bring the mixture to a boil, then reduce the heat and simmer gently for about 30 minutes.

Strain the solids out of the stock and discard them. Use the stock immediately or let it cool, then freeze.

Fish Stock

Bones and heads from a couple pounds of fish (use mild, not oily fish, such as flounder, tilefish, sea bass, or snapper), cooked or uncooked
1 medium white or yellow onion, chopped
1 medium clove garlic, chopped
2 stalks celery (with leaves, if possible), chopped
Several fresh parsley sprigs, chopped
3 to 4 whole peppercorns

If using raw fish, thoroughly rinse the bones and remove the gills. Place all the ingredients in a large stockpot and add enough water to cover them well. Bring the mixture to a boil, then reduce the heat and simmer gently for about 30 minutes.

Strain the solids out of the stock and discard them. Use the stock immediately or let it cool, then freeze.

Dashi

1 (3- to 4-inch) piece kombu (dried seaweed)
Handful of shaved dried bonito flakes
Optional add-ins: soy sauce, rice wine

Put 3 to 4 cups of water in a large pot and add the kombu. Bring to a boil, and remove the kombu just as it comes to a boil. Discard the kombu. Remove the pot from the heat and stir in the bonito flakes. Let sit for 5 minutes, or longer if you want a stronger flavor.

Strain out the bonito flakes and discard them. Stir a little soy sauce or rice wine into the broth, if you like. Use immediately or let it cool, then freeze.

Main Dishes

»»

Mexican Lasagna with Mahi

ALTERNATIVES:
swordfish, drum,
shrimp

Makes 8 servings

If you really like heat, add more chili powder and cayenne pepper, or reduce the amount for a milder flavor. To brown the cheese on top, uncover for the last 5 minutes of cooking time. When you trim the tortillas, save the scraps and make your own tortilla chips.

1½ pounds skinless, boneless mahi, cut into 1-inch chunks
2 teaspoons chili powder
1 teaspoon garlic powder
1½ teaspoons dried oregano
½ teaspoon salt
1 (16-ounce) jar tomatillo salsa
12 flour tortillas
1 (15-ounce) can black beans, rinsed and well drained
1½ cups shredded Monterey Jack cheese
Sour cream and chopped avocado for serving

Place the fish in a bowl and sprinkle with the chili powder, garlic powder, oregano, and salt. Toss to coat the fish with the seasonings. Set aside.

Preheat the oven to 350°. Lightly coat the bottom of a 9 × 13-inch baking dish with nonstick cooking spray. Spread a thin layer of the tomatillo salsa on the bottom of the dish.

Slice off part of the round sides of the tortillas to make strips that will fit in the bottom of the baking dish. Place 4 tortilla strips in the dish, covering the bottom. Spread half of the fish chunks and half of the black beans evenly over the tortilla strips. Top evenly with ½ cup of salsa and ½ cup cheese.

Place another 4 tortilla strips on top, then the rest of the fish and beans, plus ½ cup salsa and ½ cup cheese.

Place the final 4 tortilla strips on top. Spread on the remaining salsa, and top with the remaining cheese.

Cover with aluminum foil and bake for 30 minutes or until the fish is cooked through. Serve with sour cream and chopped avocado.

Oven-Roasted Dogfish with Coffee Rub

I have used a version of this rub on steaks and it's great on thick fish fillets, too. Don't use instant coffee; for the best flavor and texture, finely grind it fresh from the bean.

ALTERNATIVES:

grouper,
swordfish,
monkfish

———

Makes 4 servings

1 teaspoon smoked paprika

½ teaspoon ground ginger

1 tablespoon finely ground coffee

4½ teaspoons brown sugar

½ teaspoon ground mustard

¼ teaspoon chili powder

¼ teaspoon salt

4 meaty dogfish fillets (about 1½ pounds)

2 tablespoons vegetable oil

4 heaping teaspoons sour cream

Chopped fresh parsley for garnish

In a small bowl, combine the paprika, ginger, coffee, brown sugar, mustard, chili powder, and salt. Place the fish on a plate and rub the mixture thoroughly on both sides.

Preheat the oven to 400°. Place a cast-iron frying pan or other oven-safe pan on medium-high heat and add the oil. When the oil is hot, sprinkle the fish lightly with salt, place it in the pan, and lightly sear it, about 1 minute on each side. Do not let the rub burn. After searing both sides of the fish, place the pan in the oven and roast until the fish is cooked through, about 5 to 8 minutes.

To serve: Place the fish on a warm serving platter, top each fillet with 1 heaping teaspoon of sour cream, and sprinkle with parsley.

Fish and Chips, Tar Heel Style

ALTERNATIVES:
monkfish, grouper

Makes 6 servings

This batter on this fried fish is light and thin. Using sweet potatoes instead of conventional white potatoes gives this British favorite a North Carolina twist, since the state is the nation's top producer of sweet potatoes.

About 2 pounds sweet potatoes
1½ teaspoons chili powder, divided
½ teaspoon cumin
¼ teaspoon garlic powder
1½ teaspoons salt, divided
½ teaspoon black pepper
4 to 5 tablespoons olive oil
6 dogfish fillets (about 3 pounds)
1½ cups all-purpose flour
¾ teaspoon baking powder
1½ cups beer
Vegetable oil for frying

Peel the sweet potatoes and cut them into ½-inch thick strips. Soak the fries in cold water for at least 30 minutes, then drain and pat dry thoroughly. Preheat the oven to 400°. In a large bowl, combine 1 teaspoon of the chili powder, cumin, garlic powder, 1 teaspoon of the salt, and pepper. Add the fries and toss to coat. Oil a baking sheet with the olive oil. Spread the fries on the baking sheet in a single layer. Bake for about 30 minutes or until crispy. To promote even browning check about halfway through and stir with a spatula.

Meanwhile, prepare the fish. In a shallow dish, combine the flour, baking powder, and the remaining salt and chili powder. Add the beer and whisk to combine, eliminating any lumps. Place a frying pan on medium heat and add enough vegetable oil to come ½ inch up the sides. Heat the oil to 350° to 360° and keep at this temperature.

Dip the fish in the batter and let the excess drain off. Place the fish in the hot oil. Do not crowd the oil; you will need to work in batches. Cook the fish for 3 to 4 minutes or until lightly browned and crispy, then turn and cook the other side. When done, remove the fish to a wire rack set over a plate to catch drips and keep warm until all the fillets are cooked. Serve warm with the fries on the side.

Flatbreads with Triggerfish, Sweet Potatoes, and Chutney

The state is fortunate to have a growing number of Indian restaurants and markets, so finding garam masala and other curry powders isn't difficult. The Indian flatbread naan is also available frozen. This variation on pizza makes a fast meal. You can eat the flatbreads with a knife and fork or cut them into pieces for finger food. Turn this into an appetizer by using smaller flatbreads.

ALTERNATIVES: mahi, drum, cobia

Makes 4 servings

1½ pounds skinless triggerfish fillets, cut into 1-inch chunks

1 medium sweet potato, peeled and cut into 1-inch chunks (2 cups)

6 tablespoons olive oil, divided

1 tablespoon garam masala

Salt, to taste

1½ cups sliced white or yellow onion

4 cups fresh spinach

8 tablespoons chutney (such as Major Grey), divided

4 naans

8 to 10 fresh cilantro sprigs for garnish

Preheat the oven to 375°. Place the triggerfish and sweet potatoes in a bowl and toss with 4 tablespoons of the olive oil, the garam masala, and a pinch of salt. Spray a baking sheet with nonstick cooking spray. Spread the sweet potatoes and fish in an even layer on the pan. Bake for 20 minutes or until they are cooked through but not mushy. Remove from the oven and cover with foil to keep warm.

While the fish and sweet potatoes are cooking, place a sauté pan over medium-low heat and add the remaining olive oil. When the oil is hot, add the onions and cook, stirring, until they are lightly browned, 5 to 6 minutes. Add the spinach, lightly salt, and cook until the spinach is wilted, 2 to 3 minutes.

Heat the naans according to the package instructions.

Spread 2 tablespoons of the chutney on each of the 4 warm naans. Then evenly divide the onion-spinach mixture among the naans and top with the sweet potato and fish mixture. Garnish with cilantro sprigs.

Dogfish, Greens, and Mushroom Pasta with Cashew Butter Sauce

ALTERNATIVES: monkfish, cobia, drum

Makes 6 servings

I've loved cashews ever since I ate them hot from the dime store roaster when I was a kid. Now I'm hooked on cashew butter—same as peanut butter, but from cashews. Its sweet, nutty flavor works well with tangy greens and flavorful fish in a creamy pasta sauce that's easy to make and dairy free.

6 tablespoons cashew butter

4 tablespoons fresh lemon juice

Generous pinch of garlic powder

4 tablespoons almond or cashew milk

¼ teaspoon salt, or to taste

¼ ounce dried porcini mushrooms

8 tablespoons olive oil, divided

1½ pounds skinless dogfish fillets, cut into 1-inch cubes

3 green onions, chopped

2 medium cloves garlic, chopped

6 cups chopped fresh greens (kale, spinach, tatsoi, Chinese cabbage, or a combination)

Salt and black pepper

8 ounces hot cooked and drained penne

In a small bowl, whisk together the cashew butter, lemon juice, garlic powder, and almond or cashew milk, along with the salt. If using salted cashew butter, you may need less salt. Whisk in 3 to 4 tablespoons of water, enough to make a pourable sauce. Stir until smooth. Set aside.

Place the dried mushrooms in a small bowl, and pour in enough boiling water to cover them. Let sit for 4 to 5 minutes or until the mushrooms are soft. Drain and chop the mushrooms and set aside.

Place 4 tablespoons of the olive oil in a large sauté pan over medium-high heat. Cook the fish, stirring, until cooked through and lightly browned. Remove the fish to a large serving bowl and wipe the pan clean.

Heat the remaining olive oil in the pan, then add the mushrooms, green onions, and garlic. Cook, stirring, for 3 to 4 minutes or until the vegetables begin to soften. Add the greens and cook, stirring, until they wilt. Put the cooked vegetables in the bowl with the fish and toss to combine.

Add the hot penne to the bowl and toss, then pour in the sauce and toss to combine. Serve warm.

Greek Baked Sea Trout

ALTERNATIVES:
sheepshead,
grunt, flounder,
snapper

This recipe is a favorite at my house and is a great way to serve any flaky, medium-thick fish fillets. Cover the fillets completely with the sauce to keep them moist. You can find good cherry or grape tomatoes year-round, making them a nice choice for the sauce. Of course, the sauce will taste best with summer tomatoes.

Makes 6 servings

2 cups cherry tomatoes

½ cup chopped white or yellow onion

2 medium cloves garlic, chopped

⅓ cup olive oil, plus more for the baking pan

1 tablespoon dried oregano or marjoram

¼ teaspoon salt, or to taste

¼ teaspoon black pepper

¼ cup chopped fresh parsley

2 teaspoons capers or chopped black olives

2 large sea trout fillets (about 2 pounds)

Italian bread (optional)

Place the tomatoes in a food processor and pulse to chop coarsely. Do not purée.

Heat ⅓ cup olive oil in a large frying pan over medium heat. Add the tomatoes, onions, and garlic. Cook, stirring occasionally, until the tomatoes begin to give up their juice and the onions are soft. Add the oregano or marjoram, salt, and pepper. Reduce the heat and simmer, stirring occasionally, for about 10 minutes or until the mixture thickens slightly. Remove from the heat and stir in the parsley and capers or black olives. Taste and add salt if needed.

Preheat the oven to 350°. Coat the bottom of a baking dish with a little olive oil. Place the fish in the dish, skin-side down. Spoon the tomato sauce over the fish, making sure to cover it completely. Bake for about 20 minutes or until the fish flakes and is done.

Serve with Italian bread for sopping up the sauce, if desired.

Grilled Amberjack Tacos with Summer Corn Salsa and Chipotle Mayo

ALTERNATIVES:
triggerfish, mahi, grouper, dogfish

A neighbor was frustrated about fish tacos. She felt that the fish, which is typically fried, ends up soggy in the taco. My solution: grill it! Then add a summery salsa and mayo with a bit of heat. Use small tortillas to turn this main dish into an appetizer.

Makes 4 to 6 main
dish servings

½ cup mayonnaise

1 teaspoon adobo sauce from canned chipotles

1 teaspoon lime juice

2 pounds skinless amberjack fillets

½ teaspoon cumin

½ teaspoon salt

Vegetable oil

Corn or flour tortillas

Shredded lettuce

Summer Corn Salsa (page 168)

Shredded Monterey Jack cheese (optional)

In a small bowl, stir together the mayonnaise, adobo sauce, and lime juice. Cover and refrigerate. It can be made up to 24 hours ahead.

Cut the fish into thick chunks or finger-size strips. Put the fish in a bowl and toss with the cumin and salt. Lightly oil and heat a stovetop grill pan, or prepare a gas or charcoal grill for direct cooking. Grill the fish, turning to cook through; the length of time will depend on the thickness of the fish, but the cooking time is in minutes.

Warm tortillas according to the package directions. Assemble the tacos as follows: tortilla, shredded lettuce, fish, and Summer Corn Salsa. Top with a drizzle of the mayo. Top with cheese, if desired.

Norma's Pescado a la Veracruzana

ALTERNATIVES:
grouper, monkfish,
sea trout, flounder

Makes 4 servings

When Norma Kessler of Cary cooks this dish, it transports her back to the kitchen of her childhood home in Mexico City. Make it any time of year with canned tomatoes, but take advantage of flavorful fresh tomatoes in the summer. You could use shrimp instead of fish, but shorten the cooking time. Norma is a professional pastry chef and owner of Sweet Arielle, a bakery in Cary.

8 small whole, unpeeled Yukon Gold potatoes (about golf ball size)

¼ cup plus 1 tablespoon olive oil, divided

2½ teaspoons salt, divided

¼ teaspoon black pepper

4 black sea bass fillets (about 2 pounds)

7 medium cloves garlic, divided

1½ medium white or yellow onions, sliced, divided

1 pound fresh tomatoes, peeled and diced, retaining the juices,
     or 1 (15-ounce) can diced tomatoes, with liquid

3 bay leaves

2 fresh thyme sprigs, or 1 teaspoon dried

2 fresh marjoram or Mexican oregano sprigs, or 1 teaspoon dried

1 small stick cinnamon

3 tablespoons capers

20 to 25 green Manzanilla olives, pitted and roughly chopped

1 tablespoon chopped fresh parsley

1 (28-ounce) can peeled whole tomatoes in juice

2 to 3 medium pickled jalapeños, seeded and sliced into strips

2 tablespoons juice from pickled jalapeños

1 (8-ounce) bottle clam juice, or 1 cup fish or chicken stock

Cooked rice of your choice for serving

Chopped capers and olives (optional garnish)

Preheat the oven to 400°. Toss the potatoes with 1 tablespoon of the olive oil, ½ teaspoon of the salt, and the pepper. Spread the potatoes on a baking sheet and bake for 20 to 30 minutes or until they can be pierced easily with a fork. Turn off the heat and let them rest in the oven.

Sprinkle the fish with the remaining salt and let sit for 30 minutes to 1 hour. Salting will help the fish hold its texture.

Finely chop 2 of the garlic cloves and set aside.

Put 1the remaining olive oil in a large skillet over medium-low heat. Add 2 whole garlic cloves and cook, pressing down on the cloves with the back of a spoon, until the garlic is golden brown. Don't let it burn. Remove and discard the garlic.

Increase the heat to medium and add 1 sliced onion. Cook, stirring frequently, until translucent, 5 to 6 minutes. Add the chopped garlic, then stir and cook for another minute. Add the chopped tomatoes and their juices or the canned diced tomatoes, along with the bay leaves, thyme, marjoram or oregano, cinnamon, capers, olives, and parsley. Let the sauce simmer for 5 minutes, until it thickens slightly.

While the sauce is simmering, pour the can of whole tomatoes, the remaining garlic cloves, coarsely chopped, and the remaining onion into a blender or food processor. Purée, then pour the mixture into the simmering sauce. Stir in the jalapeños and pickling juice. Bring the sauce to a boil and add the clam juice or stock. Continue to boil for 3 minutes.

Lower the heat to a simmer, then nestle the fish into the sauce, spooning it over the fillets to cover them. Tuck the cooked potatoes into the sauce. Cover and cook about 8 minutes, until the fish is tender and cooked through. If the fillets are too large to fit all 4 in at once, cook 2 at a time and keep the first batch warm until the second is ready.

Before serving, remove the sprigs of whole herbs, bay leaves, and the cinnamon stick from the sauce. Serve the fish and sauce with cooked rice. Garnish with extra chopped olives and capers, if desired.

The Poke Bowl

Poke (pronounced po-keh) is more of a concept than a recipe. The combination of cubes of raw fish, toppings, sauce, and rice started in Hawaii and has spread across the country. I've heard it's even sold at midwestern Costcos.

I met Emma Pendergraft when I visited her journalism class at the University of North Carolina at Chapel Hill to talk about food writing. She told me how she hosted poke parties at her apartment to turn friends on to her favorite dish. "I've gotten my dad hooked, too, and he never ate any kind of raw fish before," she says.

In 2017, the Triangle got its first poke bars in Carrboro and Durham. Janet Lee, owner of ZenFish in Durham, who first ate the dish in Hawaii, says, "Poke is popular because of the grab-and-go convenience. You get something good, fast."

Here are ideas for creating your own poke bowl at home.

Fish: Because the fish will be used raw, get the absolute freshest local fish you can find, and use it immediately. Tuna is classic, but you can use other mild, firm-textured fish, such as sea bass, monkfish, or grouper. Shrimp, cooked and shelled, is another option. A half pound of fish amply serves 1 person for a meal. Use half that amount for an appetizer portion.

Preparation: Cut the fish into 1-inch cubes. It's important that the fish be bite-size. Then the question is whether to marinate, as is traditional in Hawaii, or not.

Emma marinates the diced fish overnight, covered, in the refrigerator because she likes the way it allows flavors to penetrate the fish. For ½ pound of fish, she uses 1 tablespoon of sesame oil, 1 tablespoon of soy sauce, 1 teaspoon of sesame seeds, and ¼ to ¾ teaspoon of sriracha. However, marinating will make the fish a bit chewy, and it won't have a sushi-like texture.

Janet does not marinate the fish because she wants it to have a fresh, firm texture. She puts sauce on the top when the bowl is assembled. Try it both ways and see which style appeals to you.

Toppings: Here is where you make the poke bowl your own. You can keep it simple, as Emma does, and top the tuna with cooked, shelled edamame and shredded carrots. She says that a little mayonnaise and some avocado chunks are good, too.

Janet offers a range of toppings to choose from at ZenFish, including microgreens, seaweed salad, masago (fish roe), diced cucumbers, and chopped green onions. Be sure any toppings that need to be cut up are bite-size.

Sauce: If you marinate the fish, additional sauce is probably unnecessary. Because Janet doesn't marinate, she offers several choices, such as ponzu, sweet eel sauce, sesame oil, and house-made sriracha aioli.

Assembly: Cooked rice is the base. You can use sushi rice, conventional white rice, or brown rice. Add the fish, then the toppings. If you didn't marinate the fish, add a sauce, but don't drown the bowl. Use the ingredients in proportions you like—after all, it's your poke bowl. Eat immediately.

Quick Sautéed Monkfish and Shrimp

ALTERNATIVES:
sea bass, tilefish,
triggerfish

At the end of a busy day, I needed a fast but flavorful meal. This fit the bill perfectly. Monkfish has a mild sweetness that matches great with shrimp. If you don't have spinach or want a different flavor, substitute chard or spicy arugula.

Makes 4 servings

2 tablespoons olive oil

1 tablespoon unsalted butter

½ medium white or yellow onion, chopped

2 medium cloves garlic, chopped

1½ pounds monkfish fillets, cut into ½-inch slices

8 large shrimp, peeled (devein if desired)

2 cups shredded fresh spinach

½ cup chopped fresh parsley

Salt and black pepper, to taste

Lemon wedges for serving

Heat a large sauté pan over medium heat and add the olive oil and butter. When the oil is hot and butter melted, add the onions and garlic. Cook, stirring, until they're soft but not browned, about 2 minutes.

Add the fish and shrimp. Cook, turning once or twice, until the seafood is cooked through.

Add the spinach and parsley and season with salt and pepper. Stir gently until the spinach and parsley are just wilted, about 2 minutes. Serve immediately with squeezes of lemon.

Rosefish with Young Ginger and Vadouvan Sweet Potatoes

Young, freshly picked ginger at the farmers' market pairs well with rosefish, which is moist and sweet. If you use the older, drier ginger root available in supermarkets, it may have a stronger flavor. Vadouvan is a flavorful curry powder blend that is just spicy enough without too much heat. If you can't find it, use your favorite mild curry powder.

ALTERNATIVES:
sea bass, tilefish, trout

Makes 4 servings

1 small young fresh ginger root, peeled, divided,
   or conventional fresh ginger root
⅓ cup grapeseed oil or other neutral oil
1½ pounds sweet potatoes
3 to 4 tablespoons olive oil
1 teaspoon fresh lemon juice
1 teaspoon vadouvan curry powder
Salt and black pepper, to taste
1 small bundle fresh thyme
2 pounds rosefish fillets

Cut half of the ginger into matchsticks. Place in a microwave-safe bowl and add the oil. Heat in the microwave for 15 to 20 seconds, just until warm. Set aside and let infuse for at least 1 hour.

Preheat the oven to 375°. Place the sweet potatoes in a shallow pan and roast for 45 minutes to 1 hour, until they can be easily pierced with a fork. When done, cut open and cool until they are easy to handle. Place them in a bowl and mash until smooth. Add enough olive oil to moisten them to your liking, then add the lemon juice. Stir in the vadouvan curry powder, and season with salt and pepper. Set aside and keep warm.

Heat the oven to 350°. Cut the remaining ginger into thin slices. Lightly oil a baking pan with olive oil. Make a bed of the thyme and ginger slices in the pan. Place the rosefish, skin-side down, on top of the thyme and ginger. Pour the infused oil, along with the ginger in it, over the fish. Season with salt and pepper. Bake for 10 minutes or until the fish is flaky and cooked through. Discard the thyme and ginger bed. Serve the fish alongside the sweet potatoes.

Senegalese Rice with Amberjack

ALTERNATIVES:
grouper,
sheepshead,
monkfish

Makes 6 servings

Ann Simpson of N.C. Catch, a group that advocates for and promotes the state's fishermen, got this recipe from a well-traveled friend who spent time in the African nation, where this is a traditional dish. Thanks for sharing it, Ann!

1 head garlic (about 10 cloves)

¾ cup peanut oil, divided

1 pound skinless amberjack fillets, cut into 2-inch pieces

1 large white or yellow onion, minced

4 cups chicken stock, divided

1 cup tomato paste

3 carrots, chopped

1 turnip, peeled and chopped

¼ cup fish sauce

12 whole okra pods

1 sweet potato, peeled and chopped

2 medium whole habanero peppers

Salt, to taste

2 cups long-grain white rice

Separate the head of garlic into cloves, then peel and cut each clove in half. Set aside.

In a large frying pan, heat ½ cup of the peanut oil over medium-high heat. When the oil is very hot, quickly sear the fish on each side, then remove the fish and set aside. Reduce the heat to medium and add the onions and garlic. Cook, stirring, until the vegetables are just beginning to turn golden, but don't let them brown.

Pour in 2 cups of chicken stock. Add the tomato paste and stir until dissolved. Add the carrots and turnips. Stir in the remaining 2 cups of chicken stock and the fish sauce. Bring the mixture to a boil, reduce the heat to simmer, add the fish, and cook, uncovered, for 30 minutes.

Add the okra, sweet potatoes, and habaneros. Simmer until the fish is cooked, up to 1 hour. Taste and add salt if needed, then reduce the heat to very low to keep the mixture warm.

In a separate pot, cook the rice. Ladle 3 cups of liquid from the fish mixture into the pot, then add the remaining peanut oil and bring to a boil. Add the rice, reduce the heat to a simmer, cover, and cook until the rice is done, about 20 minutes.

To serve, remove the habaneros from the fish mixture, place them in a small bowl, and mash them with a tablespoon or so of the broth to create a paste. Fluff the rice and place in a large serving platter or bowl. With a slotted spoon, remove the fish from the broth and arrange the pieces in the center of the rice. Remove the vegetables and arrange around the fish. Add a little of the broth, just enough to moisten everything. Pass the habanero paste for each diner to add as desired.

Sous-Vide Yellowfin with Herb Sauce and Farro

Restaurants have used the sous-vide method for years. The equipment cooks food in a water bath that's kept at a precise temperature, so there's no guesswork—you set the equipment to the internal temperature you want for the food, and it gently does the rest. The cooking time is longer, but it's at a lower temperature so that it doesn't overcook. It's perfect for fish. Home equipment is now available, and information on sous-vide cooking is online. The method produces tender, buttery yellowfin that is cooked to a perfect medium rare. If you use a different fish, adjust the cooking time.

ALTERNATIVES: sea bass, tuna, monkfish, swordfish

Makes 4 servings

1 handful each fresh parsley, chives, and frisée

1 thick lemon slice, seeded

Salt and black pepper, to taste

Olive oil

1½ pounds yellowfin

1 cup chicken broth

1 cup farro

2 cups chopped fresh spinach

3 green onions, chopped

2 tablespoons chopped walnuts, toasted

1 tablespoon unsalted butter (optional)

To prepare the herb sauce, place the parsley, chives, and frisée in a food processor and process until the mixture is thick but not completely smooth. Add the lemon slice and season generously with salt and pepper. With the processor running, drizzle in enough olive oil to make a thick paste. Set the sauce aside.

Begin cooking the fish according to the sous vide equipment's directions (see "Best Basics"—Sous Vide, page 20). Set the temperature at 113° to 115° for medium rare. Season the fish with salt and pepper and place in a plastic bag, then pour in a little olive oil.

While the fish is cooking, prepare the farro. Bring the chicken broth and 1 cup water to a boil. Add the farro and season with salt and pepper. Cover and simmer 30 to 40 minutes or until the liquid is absorbed and the farro is tender but still has a bite.

Heat 1 to 2 tablespoons of olive oil in a small frying pan over medium heat. Cook the spinach and green onions until wilted, 3 or 4 minutes. Stir the spinach mixture into the farro along with the chopped walnuts. Stir in the butter, if using.

When the fish is ready, remove it from the bag and pat gently with paper towels. If you'd like a crust on the surface, put a small amount of olive oil in a frying pan over medium-high heat and quickly sear the fish, just a few seconds on each side. Don't let it cook further.

To serve, place the fish on 1 or 2 spoonfuls of the farro, then spoon the herb sauce over it all.

NOTE: If you don't have sous-vide equipment, you can grill or pan-sear the fish.

Chargrilled Blackened Cape Shark Fillet over Pineapple Salsa

Cape shark, also known as dogfish, is a versatile yet little-known fish. As part of a program to encourage the consumption of underused fish, North Carolina Sea Grant enlisted chefs to develop recipes using cape shark. This sweet-spicy dish, created by chef Tim Coyne of Bistro By the Sea in Morehead City, is quick to prepare, and its tropical flavor will make you think of the beach. Several brands of blackened seasoning are available in supermarkets, and most contain salt, so you shouldn't need to add more. Tim and Sea Grant were happy to share this recipe. Rub the fish lightly with vegetable oil before adding the blackened seasoning to help the seasoning stick.

Makes 4 servings

2 cups diced fresh pineapple

1 tablespoon diced red bell pepper

2 slices pickled jalapeño

¼ cup chopped fresh cilantro, plus sprigs for garnish

Juice from 1 lime

½ teaspoon black pepper

2 tablespoons chopped fresh chives

4 cape shark fillets (about 3 ounces each)

Blackened seasoning (such as Zatarain's or Emeril's)

Prepare the salsa by combining the pineapple, bell peppers, jalapeños, chopped cilantro, lime juice, pepper, and chives in a small bowl. Set aside.

Lightly dust the fish with blackened seasoning on both sides. Preheat the oven broiler and place the fish on a nonstick baking pan or a pan sprayed with nonstick cooking spray. Broil until the fish is cooked through (see "Best Basics"—Broiling, page 15).

To serve, spoon the salsa over the cooked fish and garnish with cilantro sprigs.

NOTE: Instead of broiling, you can cook the fish on top of the stove in a sauté pan lightly coated with canola oil.

Carolina Catfish Burgers from Sweet Potatoes: A Restaurant

Makes 6 servings

Stephanie Tyson, the wonderful chef at Sweet Potatoes: A Restaurant, in my hometown of Winston-Salem, creates unusual burgers for the restaurant's burger nights. This is her favorite way to eat catfish, and may be yours, too.

FOR THE BURGERS

3 tablespoons unsalted butter

½ cup diced yellow onion

1 cup diced green bell pepper

1 teaspoon dried dill

1 teaspoon dried basil

½ teaspoon smoked paprika

3 good-size catfish fillets (5 to 6 ounces each)

1 teaspoon salt

2 to 3 dashes of hot pepper sauce (such as Tabasco or Texas Pete), optional

2 cups panko or other dry bread crumbs, divided

2 eggs, lightly beaten

1 cup vegetable oil

6 soft sandwich buns

Lettuce, sliced tomatoes, and Classic Creamy Slaw (page 162)

FOR THE CHILI MAYONNAISE

1 cup mayonnaise

2 teaspoons lime juice

2 teaspoons chili powder

1 teaspoon cumin

¼ cup ketchup

Put the butter in a medium skillet over medium heat. Add the onions, bell peppers, dill, basil, and paprika. Cook, stirring, until the vegetables are soft but not mushy, 3 to 4 minutes. Remove from the heat.

In a larger skillet, add the catfish and salt with enough water to cover. Bring to a boil, cover, and lower the heat to simmer. Cook until the fish is done, 7 to 8 minutes. Remove from the heat and drain. Remove any skin or stray bones. Place the fish in a mixing bowl and allow to cool. Add the onion mixture and mix well, breaking up the fish as you stir. Add the hot pepper sauce, if using, then fold in 1½ cups of the panko and the eggs. Mix thoroughly.

Place the remaining panko on a plate. Form the fish mixture into ½-cup patties and roll them in the panko. Heat the vegetable oil in a large skillet over medium heat and add the catfish burgers. Cook for about 3 minutes or until browned on one side, then turn over and continue cooking until the burgers are firm to the touch and heated through.

For the chili mayonnaise, combine the ingredients in a small mixing bowl.

Toast the sandwich buns and spread them with chili mayonnaise. Add lettuce, tomatoes, and the catfish burgers. Top with Classic Creamy Slaw.

Grilled Drum Steaks with Apple Salsa

ALTERNATIVES:
wahoo, cobia,
swordfish

Makes 4 servings

Fruit salsas go great with grilled fish, but most use summer fruits. On a fall day, I wanted a flavor to match the season. Grilling apples adds a smoky taste and concentrates their sweetness, so be sure to use a tart or tangy apple variety such as Cameo, Winesap, or Granny Smith. Taste the apples first and adjust the amount of honey depending on their sweetness.

2 firm apples, cored and thickly sliced
2 green onions, cut into pieces
1 medium mild green pepper (sweet banana or Giant Marconi),
    halved and seeded
Grapeseed or other neutral oil
2 tablespoons apple cider vinegar
1 tablespoon fresh lemon juice
1 teaspoon honey
Salt and black pepper, to taste
¼ teaspoon powdered mustard
2 teaspoons olive oil, divided
1 tablespoon chopped fresh chives or parsley
4 drum steaks (about 2 pounds)
1 teaspoon sherry vinegar

Prepare a gas or charcoal grill for direct cooking. Spray a grill pan with nonstick spray and place it on the grill to heat. Toss the apples, green onions, and peppers in a small amount of neutral oil. Place them on the grill pan and grill, turning occasionally, for a few minutes until they are lightly charred but still firm. Do not overcook the apples. Let everything cool until you can handle them, then coarsely chop them and put them in a bowl.

In a small bowl, whisk together the apple cider vinegar, lemon juice, honey, salt, pepper, powdered mustard, and 1 teaspoon of the olive oil. Stir in the chives or parsley. Pour the mixture over the apple combination and toss to coat. Set aside.

Rub the fish steaks with the sherry vinegar and the remaining olive oil, then season with salt and pepper. Do this no more than 5 minutes before cooking. Grill over direct heat, turning once, until the fish is cooked through. (see "Best Basics"—Grilling, page 17.)

Serve the fish topped with the apple salsa.

MAIN DISHES

Charcoaled Mullet

If you've only encountered fish on ice in an inland market, you likely don't know mullet, which is also called fat mullet, striped mullet, or jumping mullet. But read cookbooks from coastal churches and communities and you'll usually find recipes for cooking the bony fish or its roe by grilling or smoking—and it has a strong flavor. Historically, "mullet barbecues" over open fires were times for community fellowship. Mullet is high in fish oil, the healthy stuff people take pills to get, so some restaurant chefs are beginning to explore it. Grilling and smoking are great ways to cook higher-oil fish in general. Most charcoaled mullet recipes are similar, saying to grill over charcoal for the smoky goodness. Traditionally the fish is cooked whole. This recipe is a combination of ones from several historical sources.

Serves 1 fish per person

Cleaned whole mullets

Salt and black pepper

Lemon juice, chopped watermelon, or
  vinegar-based barbecue sauce

Liberally salt and pepper the fish. Get a charcoal grill going, or use an open fire with the wood burned down to coals.

If using a charcoal grill, place the whole fish on the grill grate. If using an open fire, insert a stick or stake lengthwise into the fish. Leave the fish at the end and stick the stake into the ground so that the fish will extend over the coals and cook.

Cooking time will depend on the size of the fish, from 20 to 30 minutes. Pass around the lemon juice, chopped watermelon, or barbecue sauce to serve on top.

Tim's Grilled Fat Mullet in Sorghum-Soy Sauce

ALTERNATIVE:
bluefish

Makes 4 servings

Tim Lucas of Raleigh works at the Nicholas School of the Environment at Duke University, where in 2009 he helped students establish one of the state's first community-supported fisheries, Walking Fish. Subscribers were reluctant to try fat mullet, also known as jumping mullet or striped mullet, a high-oil fish with a strong flavor that's an old-time coastal favorite. He brought home some unclaimed fillets and paired them with other assertive flavors, and his family has been savoring this fish ever since.

½ cup sorghum syrup
½ cup soy sauce
6 ounces pineapple juice
½ teaspoon sesame oil
1 teaspoon sriracha, or to taste
1 teaspoon minced garlic
1 teaspoon kosher salt
Zest of 1 lemon (quarter the lemon for garnish and reserve)
4 fat mullet fillets (about 3½ to 4 pounds before trimming)
Minced fresh chives for garnish
Cooked rice of your choice or barley for serving

Combine the sorghum, soy sauce, pineapple juice, sesame oil, sriracha, garlic, salt, and lemon zest in a resealable plastic bag. Seal the bag and shake a few times to combine the ingredients. Open the bag and add the fish. Press out the excess air, seal, and refrigerate, at least 2 hours or up to 6 hours.

Prepare a charcoal or gas grill for direct cooking. Remove the fish from the marinade, reserving the marinade. Allow the fish to come to room temperature. Pour the reserved marinade into a small saucepan. Bring it to a rolling boil, then lower the heat and simmer until the marinade is reduced by half. Remove from the heat and cover to keep warm.

Place the fish on the grill, skin-side down. Cook for 6 to 8 minutes, until the skin is crisp and the flesh is just firm. Do not turn over the fish. Transfer to a serving platter, drizzle with the reduced marinade, and sprinkle with minced chives. Serve with lemon wedges and your favorite grain, such as rice or barley, with the remaining sauce on the side.

NOTE: If you don't like the skin, give it to your dogs, who will think you are brilliant.

18 Seaboard's Carolina Classics Cornmeal-Crusted Catfish with Herbed Grits Cakes

Makes 10 servings

Chef Jason Smith in Raleigh was an early evangelist for North Carolina fish and seafood. "Using North Carolina seafood is the only way to go. It's sustainable and it's good," he says. He particularly likes farm-raised catfish from Carolina Classics in Ayden. Diners like it, too; this dish is a mainstay of the menu at 18 Seaboard, the Raleigh flagship of his restaurant collection that now includes Cantina 18 and Harvest 18. I'm grateful to Jason for sharing the recipe. Note: You can prepare the grits cakes up to 1 day ahead and refrigerate. Prepare the champagne vinegar-tarragon butter just before beginning to fry the catfish.

FOR THE GRITS CAKES

10 cups water

2 cups heavy cream

4 cups grits

½ bunch fresh parsley, chopped

½ cup sliced fresh basil

Salt and black pepper, to taste

FOR THE BUTTER

½ shallot, chopped

2 fresh tarragon sprigs

3 black peppercorns

1 cup white wine

¼ cup champagne vinegar

1 cup (2 sticks) unsalted butter, melted

½ teaspoon salt

¼ teaspoon white pepper

FOR THE FISH

10 catfish fillets (about 7 ounces each)

Cornmeal for dredging

Salt and black pepper, to taste

2 tablespoons olive oil

For the grits cakes, in a large saucepan, bring the water and cream to a boil, then reduce the heat to medium low and stir in the grits. Cook, stirring frequently, until the grits are firm. Remove from the heat, stir in the parsley and basil, and season with salt and black pepper. Cover a sheet pan with parchment paper, then spread the grits on in a smooth layer. Let cool, then cut into 20 triangles.

This can be done a day ahead, and the triangles can be covered and refrigerated. Lightly pan-grill the triangles before serving.

Just before beginning to fry the catfish, prepare the champagne vinegar-tarragon butter: Combine the shallots, tarragon, peppercorns, white wine, and champagne vinegar in a saucepan and bring to a boil. Reduce heat to a simmer, then simmer until the mixture is reduced by half. Strain the liquid and pour into a blender (don't fill it more than half full; you may have to work in batches). Blend, slowly adding the butter to emulsify. Taste, then add salt and white pepper as needed.

When ready to cook the catfish, season the fillets with salt and black pepper. Coat the belly side of the fish only in cornmeal (do not coat the skin side). Heat the oil in a cast-iron skillet on medium heat, place the fish cornmeal-side down in the hot oil, let it cook for 3 minutes, flip, and finish cooking for another 4 minutes. Let the fish drain on a rack over a plate.

Remove the grits cakes from the refrigerator and lightly pan-grill to reheat.

To assemble the dish, place 2 grits cakes on a plate, place 1 piece of fish on top, and drizzle with the butter.

Jon's Spicy Bluefish Tacos

Makes 6 servings

I confessed to my friend Jon Whatley in Raleigh that I've never been crazy about bluefish. As a devoted fisherman and a good cook, he took my statement as a challenge, and here's the result. Jon cooks whole fish that he's just pulled from the water, but landlubbers can use fillets. Either way, Jon says the key is to be sure the bluefish is extremely fresh and properly handled to avoid a strong flavor. It pays to know your fishmonger or have a fishing friend. Since the purpose of this recipe is to give bluefish some love, I'm not offering alternative choices—give the fish a chance!

3 medium to large whole, cleaned bluefish,
    or 6 bluefish fillets (about 2 pounds)
4 tablespoons unsalted butter, melted
1 tablespoon olive oil
1 medium clove garlic, crushed
Sriracha, to taste
Kosher salt, to taste
Fresh lemon juice, to taste
½ head cabbage, thinly sliced
½ medium sweet onion, thinly sliced
4 tablespoons mayonnaise
3 tablespoons red wine vinegar
1½ tablespoons sugar
1 large tomato, thinly sliced
1 large cucumber, thinly sliced
12 (1 package) soft flour tortillas
Shredded cheddar cheese
Sour cream

Place each whole fish on a large sheet of heavy-duty aluminum foil. (If using fillets, you could put 2 fillets in each packet.) Mix the melted butter with the olive oil, crushed garlic, and sriracha. Sprinkle the fish with salt and squeeze on lemon juice. Spread the butter mixture over the fish and tightly seal the foil.

Prepare a grill for medium-high heat. Place the foil packets on the preheated grill. Cook for 8 minutes, then turn over the packets, being careful not to tear the foil, and cook for 8 minutes more, a total of 16 minutes. Remove the packets from the heat but leave them sealed while you prepare the other ingredients.

Place the cabbage and onions in a large mixing bowl. In a separate bowl, mix the mayonnaise, vinegar, and sugar. Adjust the sauce to your taste, using more or less sugar and vinegar. Pour the sauce into the cabbage mixture and stir well.

Open the foil packets and use a fork to carefully flake the fish away from the bones, discarding the bones and skin. Make sure to check for small bones.

To assemble the tacos, place a tortilla on a plate. Use tongs to place some of the cabbage mixture on the tortilla, then add some fish, tomato slices, and cucumber slices. Top with cheese and sour cream.

Nancie's Steamed Whole Flounder with Cilantro, Green Onions, and Fresh Ginger

ALTERNATIVES:
black bass, striped bass, snapper

Makes 4 servings

Nancie McDermott of Chapel Hill has written a plethora of cookbooks about both southern and Asian food. Her time with the Peace Corps in Thailand has made food from that part of the world especially dear to her. Nancie graciously shared her recipe for a traditional Asian method of cooking whole fish in a wok.

1 (1½- to 2-pound) whole flounder, cleaned and scaled,
    with head and tail left on
1 large bunch green onions
½ cup thinly sliced fresh ginger, divided (no need to peel)
⅓ cup soy sauce
⅓ cup vegetable oil
1 cup fresh cilantro sprigs
Cooked rice of your choice for serving

Prepare the fish by cutting 3 diagonal slits, about 2 inches apart, through the skin on each side. Place the fish on a heatproof platter or plate that is deep enough to hold the liquid, which will accumulate as the fish cooks. Set aside.

Prepare the green onions: Trim away the rough top ends and root ends. Chop the onions in half and separate the white and green portions. Carefully chop each half into 2-inch sections. Cut each section lengthwise into very thin strips. Toss the strips in a bowl to fluff them up into a haystack. You should have ½ cup of chopped onions. Set aside.

Prepare a wok or very large pan for steaming and place a steaming rack in it. (See Note.) The rack will hold the heatproof platter on which the fish will steam. Pour 3 inches of water into the wok. Sprinkle half of the ginger over the fish. Place the platter with the fish on the rack inside the wok and turn the heat to high. When the water is steaming actively, adjust the heat to maintain a lively flow of steam. Cover and begin timing. Steam the fish for 10 minutes. Check and add water if necessary.

Meanwhile, heat the soy sauce in a microwave or in a small pan on top of the stove until very hot. Set aside.

At the end of 10 minutes, remove the cover and check the fish for doneness (be careful of the hot steam). Very gently lift a chunk of meat away from the bone in the thickest part of the fish. The meat should be opaque, firm, and just done. Turn off the heat. When the steam subsides, carefully lift out the platter using oven mitts and gently tilt it toward the sink to pour off liquid that accumulated during steaming. Cover the fish to keep warm.

In a small pan or skillet, heat the vegetable oil until very hot. Pour the hot soy sauce over the fish. Scatter the remaining ginger and all the green onion shreds on the fish. Then carefully pour the hot oil over the fish, which will sizzle and hiss as the oil hits. Sprinkle the cilantro over it all. Serve immediately with rice. See instructions for filleting whole cooked fish in "Best Basics," page 17.

NOTE: If you don't have a wok, try a large pan that's wide enough to accommodate a baking rack and the whole fish. You may need to change the amount of water depending on the size of the pan.

Tilefish Maque Choux

ALTERNATIVES:
trout, catfish,
sheepshead

Makes 4 servings

Maque choux is a traditional Louisiana dish, and I have concocted a version that is a great home for sweet, flaky tilefish. Use fresh corn if it's in season, but frozen will work, too.

4 slices bacon

2 pounds tilefish fillets

Salt and black pepper, to taste

1 cup chopped red onion

1 cup chopped red or green bell pepper

4 medium cloves garlic, chopped

4 cups corn kernels

2 cups chopped tomatoes

1 teaspoon dried thyme

2 teaspoons dried marjoram or oregano

Place a large frying pan over medium heat and cook the bacon until crispy. Drain the bacon on paper towels, then crumble and set aside. Reserve the pan and bacon grease.

Put about 2 tablespoons of the bacon grease into a second frying pan over medium-high heat. Season the fish with salt and pepper, and place in the hot pan. Briefly sear the fish on each side, until lightly browned. Set the fish aside off the heat.

Place the first frying pan with the remaining bacon grease on medium-high heat. Add the red onions and bell peppers, and sauté until they begin to soften, about 2 minutes. Add the garlic, corn, tomatoes, thyme, and marjoram or oregano, and season with salt. Sauté for 2 to 3 minutes or until the corn is soft and the tomatoes begin to give off liquid (you may add 1 or 2 tablespoons of water to speed the process). Add a little olive oil if the vegetables start to stick to the pan.

Reduce the heat to medium and nestle the fish into the mixture. Cover the pan and cook for 4 to 5 minutes or until the fish is cooked through. Sprinkle the crumbled bacon on top and serve.

Orange-Ginger Snapper

This recipe contains three of my favorite things: ginger, garlic, and citrus. And it cooks up quick—I've made it for an indulgent lunch. Serve with a salad and rice pilaf.

ALTERNATIVES:
perch, flounder, trout

Makes 4 servings

4 to 6 tablespoons unsalted butter
1⅓ pounds red snapper fillets
Salt and black pepper
4 teaspoons finely chopped garlic
4 teaspoons finely chopped fresh ginger
2 teaspoons grated orange zest
4 tablespoons orange juice
2 tablespoons Grand Marnier or other orange liqueur
Chopped fresh basil or parsley for garnish

Place a large sauté pan on medium-high heat and add the butter. Season both sides of the fish with salt and pepper. When the butter is hot, sear the fish quickly on each side, then place on a plate and keep warm.

Add more butter if there isn't enough to coat the bottom of the pan and reheat. Add the garlic and ginger and cook, stirring for a minute or so. Don't let it brown. Add the orange zest, orange juice, and Grand Marnier, stir, and reduce the heat to medium low. Simmer the sauce for 1 to 2 minutes until it thickens slightly.

Return the fish to the pan and cook for another couple of minutes, spooning the sauce over it, until the fish is cooked through. Remove to a plate and garnish with basil or parsley.

Panko-Crusted Shichimi Togarashi Triggerfish

ALTERNATIVES:
dogfish, grunt,
sheepshead

———

Makes 4 servings

In a Japanese market, I picked up shichimi togarashi, a seven-spice blend often used as a condiment for soup or noodles. It's a great seasoning for fish. Shredded nori would add another flavor and texture to this dish.

4 triggerfish fillets (about 2 pounds)
Salt, to taste
2 eggs, beaten
3 teaspoons shichimi togarashi
½ teaspoon ground ginger
½ teaspoon toasted sesame seeds
2 cups panko
Vegetable oil
Shredded nori (optional)

Place the fish on a plate and season on both sides with salt. Dip each fillet into the egg, let the excess egg drip off, then place on the plate. Sprinkle with the togarashi, ginger, and sesame seeds.

Heat a large sauté pan over medium heat and add enough oil to cover the bottom. When the oil is hot, gently roll the fillets in the panko and place them in the pan. Fry for about 2 minutes, until the bottom begins to brown, then turn over the fillets and fry until cooked through. Adjust the heat if necessary to prevent the panko from burning. Turn the fillets gently to keep the panko from coming off; a fish spatula is helpful (see "Best Basics"—Frying, page 16). Sprinkle with shredded nori, if using, and serve warm.

Pecan-Crusted Catfish in Bourbon Cream Sauce

ALTERNATIVES:
trout, flounder,
striped bass

This recipe is full of classic southern ingredients: buttermilk, pecans, bourbon, and catfish. A short soak in buttermilk improves the texture of the fish and makes the coating adhere. Use a food processor or blender to chop the pecans into the consistency of coarse cornmeal.

Makes 4 servings

2 pounds catfish fillets, cut into 4 pieces

1 cup buttermilk

1 cup finely chopped pecans

½ cup all-purpose flour

¼ teaspoon salt

10 tablespoons unsalted butter, divided

1 teaspoon chopped garlic

4 tablespoons bourbon

2 teaspoons grated lemon zest

½ cup half-and-half

Chopped fresh parsley for garnish

Pour the buttermilk into a large, shallow dish and add the fish, turning to coat. Let sit for 15 minutes.

In a large, shallow dish, combine the chopped pecans, flour, and salt. When the fish has finished soaking, remove it from the buttermilk, letting any excess drip off, then coat in the pecan mixture.

Place a large sauté pan over medium heat and add 5 tablespoons of the butter. Cook the fillets for about 4 minutes on each side or until they flake easily and are cooked through. Adjust the heat if necessary to keep the coating from burning. Remove the fish, place on a plate and cover with foil or put in an oven on low heat to keep warm.

Using a clean sauté pan over medium heat, heat the remaining butter. Add the garlic and cook, stirring, for about 1 minute or just until the garlic becomes fragrant. Stir in the bourbon, then the lemon zest. Cook, stirring constantly, for 1 to 2 minutes or until the mixture thickens. Reduce the heat to medium low and stir in the half-and-half. Cook, stirring constantly, for another 1 to 2 minutes, until the sauce thickens.

To serve, place the fish on individual serving plates and drizzle the sauce over, then sprinkle with parsley.

How to Throw a Fish Fry

Fish frys are classics for church fund-raisers or family reunions. But there's more to a fish fry than just heating a big pot of oil and throwing fish in it. Pastor Roger Hayes of Winston-Salem has been holding fish frys for many years to raise money for his church, Church of the Holy Spirit Fellowship, plus other organizations. He also cooks for college homecoming celebrations, family reunions, and parties. In November 2016, he took his cooking skills on the road with a food truck, Wutyasay: Good Food That Makes the Soul Smile.

"Fish frys are popular because it's a communal thing, people enjoy coming together," Roger says. "The aroma and the waiting process turns into fellowship, which turns into conversation."

Here are Roger's tips for organizing a fish fry.

- The right equipment is vital, as is outdoor space. This is not an indoor activity. Be sure to place the fryer away from flammable material, and don't leave it unattended. Using a large pot on a propane burner is OK, but sediment will eventually fall to the bottom and burn. You'll have to replace and reheat the oil if you are cooking for a large group. Roger uses a propane-fueled fryer specially made for fish with a V-bottom design that allows sediment to fall into cooler oil below the heating element. The sediment doesn't burn and the oil stays clean. "The right equipment took me to a whole other level," Roger says.

- Use a cooking thermometer to keep the oil at the proper temperature. Too-cool oil causes greasy results. The oil should be at a consistent 350° as you cook. If the oil gets dirty or sediment burns, you must replace it with fresh oil. Fill the pot and heat the oil according to the fryer manufacturer's directions. Wear a heavy apron to protect clothing from oil spatters, and don't leave the fryer unattended.

- Before you begin frying, have tongs, a sieve, or a fry basket at hand to remove the fish as it cooks. Also have a large pan lined with paper towels nearby to hold the cooked fish. The fish will cook quickly, in mere minutes.

- Use firm, mild white fish fillets such as whiting (also called sea mullet), catfish, perch, or striped bass. Roger likes whole croaker if he's cooking for his family. Using 4-ounce fillets, 10 to 12 pounds of fish would feed a dozen people along with side dishes.

- He recommends that the fish be slightly cool, not at room temperature, when you bread and fry it, for better texture. If using frozen fish, thaw it but keep it cold. Gently dry the fish with paper towels before rolling it in the breading to prevent the breading from clumping.

- After proper oil temperature, it's all about the breading, Roger says. He prefers breading without cornmeal and likes it a little spicy. "I want it to give the flavoring I want and a good presentation," he says. He does not dip the fish in egg before breading it because he thinks that darkens the oil and the fish unattractively.

- Shake off excess breading before placing the fish into the hot oil a few pieces at a time. Don't overload the fryer to keep the oil temperature from falling and the fish from clumping together. It will take just 4 minutes to cook a 4-ounce fillet. Remove the fish from the oil and let drain well in the pan lined with paper towels.

- Roger says that the two essential sides for a fish fry are coleslaw and tartar sauce. He may serve baked beans and macaroni and cheese as well. "That's the best meal this side of heaven," he says. The pastor ought to know.

Roger's Spicy Fish Breading

Roger Hayes kindly shared his easy breading recipe. It can be made ahead and stored in an airtight container; stir before using. Note that both the breading mix and the lemon-pepper seasoning contain salt, so you won't need to add any to the recipe.

1 (2-pound) bag seafood breading mix
  (Roger uses House-Autry brand)
3 tablespoons lemon-pepper seasoning
3 tablespoons granulated garlic (do not use garlic salt)
2 tablespoons Mrs. Dash Extra Spicy Seasoning Blend

Combine all the ingredients in a large bowl. Use immediately or store in an airtight container.

Simple Roasted Whole Black Sea Bass

Chefs love whole fish, saying that the bones add flavor in much the same way that bone-in chicken is more flavorful. The idea of serving a whole fish can freak out home cooks, but it's easy. Try it and you'll enjoy some of the most moist and flavorful fish you've ever prepared.

ALTERNATIVES:
sheepshead, snapper, trout

———
Makes 4 servings

2 (1 to 1½-pound) whole black sea bass, cleaned and scaled,
  with head and tail left on
6 to 8 fresh cilantro sprigs
6 small fresh ginger slices
4 thin lime or lemon slices
Olive oil
Salt and black pepper, to taste

Preheat the oven to 350°.

Oil a baking tray well and place the fish on it. Place 3 or 4 cilantro sprigs in each fish along with 3 ginger slices and 2 lime slices. Don't overstuff the fish; use less if the fish is small. Drizzle olive oil over the fish and season with salt and pepper.

Place the fish in the oven and bake for 20 to 30 minutes or until the fish tests done.

For how to separate fillets and serve, see "Best Basics"—Filleting, page 17.

Striped Bass with Spring Salad

ALTERNATIVES:
trout, perch,
tilefish

Makes 6 servings

I was craving fresh flavors on an early spring day and came up with this recipe. Pea tips (also called pea greens) are a type of snow pea grown for the green tops, and they have a sweet flavor. Look for them in Asian markets.

2 cups shredded fresh pea tips

3 green onions, white parts only

2 tablespoons grapeseed or other neutral oil

1½ teaspoons fresh lemon juice

1 thumb-size knob fresh ginger, peeled

½ teaspoon salt, plus more to taste, divided

¼ teaspoon black pepper, plus more to taste, divided

1½ pounds striped bass fillets

4 tablespoons olive oil, divided

¼ cup chopped white or yellow onion

1 tablespoon chopped fresh chives

3 tablespoons sherry vinegar

Place the shredded pea tips in a large bowl. Cut the green onions lengthwise and separate into long shreds. Toss with the pea tips.

Put the oil and lemon juice in a separate small bowl. Cut the ginger into chunks and place in a garlic press. Use the press to squeeze juice from the ginger into the mixture of oil and lemon juice; you should get about ¼ teaspoon. Add ½ teaspoon of salt and ¼ teaspoon of pepper, and whisk to combine. Pour over the greens and toss. Use just enough vinaigrette to coat the leaves. Set aside.

Put 2 tablespoons of the olive oil in a large frying pan over medium heat. Season the fish with salt and pepper. Place the fillets in the pan, skin-side down, and cook about 2 minutes per side or until the fish flakes and is done. Adjust the heat depending on the size of your fillets; thicker ones will need lower heat. Place the fillets on a platter and keep warm.

Scrape any skin or bits that might burn from the pan. Add the remaining olive oil and place on medium-high heat. Add the onions and cook until soft. Add the chives and sherry vinegar. Raise the heat and simmer, stirring, until the mixture thickens, about 1 minute. Pour the sauce over the fillets.

To serve, divide the salad among 6 plates, then top each plate with a piece of the fish and its sauce.

Crunchy Baked Trout with Arugula Salad

ALTERNATIVES: catfish, striped bass, flounder

Makes 4 servings

Ben Barker in Chapel Hill, chef of the beloved Magnolia Grill, gave me the idea for cooking fish in mayonnaise. I added a crunchy coating to contrast with the rich, tender fish, and it was delicious. Ben has never steered me wrong. As for the kind of mayo to use, it's up to your conscience, but as good southerners, Ben and I use Duke's.

FOR THE FISH

1 teaspoon fresh lemon juice

½ cup mayonnaise

2 teaspoons Dijon mustard

¾ teaspoon black pepper

2 cups unsweetened plain cornflakes

4 trout fillets (about 2 pounds)

Salt, to taste

FOR THE SALAD

2½ cups arugula

⅔ cup coarsely chopped fresh Italian parsley

4 teaspoons fresh lemon juice

6 teaspoons olive oil

2 teaspoons capers

½ teaspoon black pepper

½ teaspoon salt

For the fish: Preheat the oven to 375°. Spray a baking pan with nonstick cooking spray. In a small bowl, combine the lemon juice, mayonnaise, mustard, and pepper. In another bowl, lightly crush the cornflakes with your hands; don't overcrush them, but leave them in pieces.

Lightly coat the bottom of the baking pan with olive oil. Place the fish skin-side down in the pan and sprinkle with salt. Coat each fillet with the mayonnaise mixture, being sure to cover all the fish with a light layer. Lightly press the cornflakes into the mayonnaise coating. Place the pan in the oven and bake for 10 to 12 minutes or until the fish is done and the cornflakes are lightly browned; don't let them burn.

While the fish is baking, prepare the salad: In a bowl toss together the arugula and parsley with the lemon juice, olive oil, capers, pepper and salt.

To serve, divide the salad among 4 plates, then top each plate with a fillet.

Sunburst Trout Farms, Waynesville

SEVEN DECADES OF A FISHY FAMILY BUSINESS

This rainbow trout farm in the mountains near Asheville has been around, operated by the same family, for almost seventy years. It sells fresh fillets to restaurants and fish markets as far west as Texas. Also, they've done about everything you can do with trout: cold smoked trout, trout sausage, trout jerky, trout pastrami, trout caviar.

Trout is the family business, and the indoctrination starts early. Anna Eason, marketing director, says she fed trout caviar to her kids when they were toddlers.

Sunburst Trout cuts 500,000 pounds of fresh trout a year. North Carolina as a whole is second in the country in trout production, after Idaho.

The company purchases four-ounce fingerlings from a local hatchery and raises them to two-pound fish in about eighteen months. In nearby Canton the fish grow in a series of raceways that are fed by 55° mountain water. Trout like to swim upstream like salmon, Eason says. Water temperature is crucial. "If it's a cold winter, they won't eat, and heat stresses them out," she says. "In the hot part of the summer, we'll send the fish to a farm at a higher elevation. In 72° water, the fish will go belly-up."

A boom truck with a huge net harvests the fish and brings them to holding ponds for processing in Waynesville. Each fish yields two eight-ounce fillets.

Rainbow trout is not native to the state, but the species is better for farming than the native brown trout. Eason says that a natural yeast is added to the food to give the fillets the light pink color that consumers expect.

Monterey Bay Seafood Watch rates farmed trout a "Best Choice" because environmentally responsible methods to control pollution are widely used and the industry is effectively regulated.

Eason says that at Sunburst, the used water is filtered and placed in settling ponds. Waste falls to the bottom and is left behind when the clean water on top is released to a river. The waste, plus other waste from fish processing, is composted. "Farmers come to get it for fertilizer. And I have the best garden in the neighborhood," she says.

For more information, visit sunburst trout.com.

Tailgate Seafood Mixed Grill

Brats and fried chicken are the usual tailgate foods. But in Hawaii, football fans use the islands' abundant seafood for pregame meals. A version of this recipe appeared in my book *Fan Fare: A Playbook of Great Recipes for Tailgating or Watching the Game at Home*.

¼ cup bottled clam juice

½ pound choy sum or spinach

½ pound baby bok choy

2 to 3 pounds snapper fillets, cut into 3-ounce pieces

1 pound littleneck clams, rinsed well

1 pound medium shrimp in the shell

8 tablespoons (1 stick) unsalted butter, cut into pats

2 lemons

1 tablespoon chopped garlic

1 medium tomato, diced

¼ cup dry white wine

Dash of soy sauce

Salt and black pepper, to taste

Prepare a charcoal or gas grill for direct cooking.

Combine the clam juice with ¼ cup water and pour into a 9 × 13-inch disposable foil pan. Tear the choy sum and baby bok choy into individual leaves (leave spinach leaves whole, if using) and arrange them evenly on the bottom of the pan. Place the snapper near the center of the pan. Arrange the clams around the snapper and the shrimp on top of the fish. Evenly place pats of butter on top of the seafood. Thinly slice 1 lemon and arrange on top of the butter. Sprinkle everything with the garlic, tomato, white wine, and soy sauce. Season lightly with salt and pepper.

Cover the pan tightly with aluminum foil to steam the seafood. Place the pan on the grill. Cook for 5 to 7 minutes (the foil will puff up after about 2 minutes; this is normal) or until the fish flakes easily with a fork and the clams have opened slightly. Slice the second lemon and garnish the dish before serving.

Sweet Potato–Crusted Sea Mullet with Pomegranate Vinaigrette

ALTERNATIVES:
sheepshead, sea bass, sea trout

Makes 4 servings

My Raleigh friend Oona Lewis and her husband ate a fish dish using sweet potatoes while on vacation and liked it so much that they re-created it at home. This is my version of her idea. The richness of the sweet potato and sea mullet asks for a little zing. If you don't have pomegranate juice to make the vinaigrette, a simple squeeze of fresh lemon is good, too. Use a food processor to chop the sweet potato quickly into medium-size pieces, but don't chop it too finely to keep a crunchy texture.

1 cup all-purpose flour

¼ teaspoon dried sage

½ teaspoon dried thyme

Salt and black pepper, to taste

2 eggs, beaten

2 cups peeled, medium-chopped sweet potato

1 cup cornmeal

1½ pounds sea mullet fillets

Vegetable oil

2 tablespoons pomegranate juice

1 tablespoon fresh lemon juice

3 tablespoons olive oil

Pinch of sugar, or to taste

In a shallow bowl, combine the flour, sage, thyme, salt, and pepper. Place the beaten eggs in another bowl. In a third shallow bowl, combine the chopped sweet potato and cornmeal.

Place a large sauté pan over medium-high heat and add enough oil to cover the bottom. Dredge the fish first in the seasoned flour, then in the egg, then in the sweet potato–cornmeal mixture. Place the fish in the pan skin-side down and cook for about 1 minute, until lightly browned. Carefully turn over and cook the other side, lightly browning each side.

Preheat the oven to 375°. Lift the fish from the sauté pan, trying not to lose any coating, and place skin-side down on a nonstick baking sheet (or a sheet sprayed with nonstick cooking spray). Bake for 5 to 8 minutes or until the fish flakes easily and is cooked through.

While the fish bakes, whisk the pomegranate juice, lemon juice, olive oil, and pinch of sugar, along with salt and pepper to taste, in a small bowl.

When the fish is done, drizzle lightly with the vinaigrette and serve.

Sweet-Spicy Glazed Triggerfish with Butternut Squash Noodles

ALTERNATIVES:
catfish, sea trout,
flounder

You've probably seen noodles made from butternut squash. Although I wouldn't serve marinara sauce on them, they're a refreshing change from potatoes and pasta. This quick glaze for fish brings out their sweetness. The noodles cook fast, so wait until the fish is nearly or even completely done to start them.

Makes 4 servings

¼ cup peach jam

1 teaspoon grated orange zest

3 tablespoons orange juice

1 teaspoon fresh lemon juice

¼ teaspoon hot pepper sauce (such as Tabasco or Texas Pete), or to taste

Generous dash of ground nutmeg

Scant ¼ teaspoon ground cloves

Dash of salt

1 tablespoon grapeseed or other neutral oil

4 triggerfish fillets (about 1¼ pounds)

Olive oil

3 green onions, chopped

1 medium clove garlic, chopped

1 (10.7-ounce) container butternut squash noodles

Snow pea sprouts for garnish (optional)

Preheat the oven to 375°. Coat a baking pan with nonstick cooking spray.

In a small saucepan, combine the peach jam, orange zest, orange juice, and lemon juice. Place the saucepan over low heat and warm, stirring, until the jam melts and combines with the juices. Remove from the heat and stir in the hot pepper sauce, nutmeg, cloves, and salt. Whisk the oil into the mixture until smooth.

Place the fish, skin-side down, in the baking pan and spread the jam mixture over it, covering the fish. Bake for about 15 minutes or until the fish flakes and is done.

Near the end of the fish's cooking time, prepare the butternut squash noodles. Place a large sauté pan over medium heat and add enough olive oil to cover the bottom. Add the green onions and garlic, salt lightly, and cook, stirring, until the onions begin to get soft. Add the noodles and cook, stirring, until they soften, 3 to 4 minutes.

To serve, divide the noodle mixture among 4 plates, place a piece of fish on top of each, and garnish with snow pea sprouts, if desired.

Seafood Tetrazzini

This baked pasta dish isn't as rich as typical turkey or chicken tetrazzini. Using milk instead of cream offers a lighter flavor that goes perfectly with the seafood.

ALTERNATIVES: flounder, triggerfish, trout

Makes 8 servings

1 pound spaghetti

5 tablespoons unsalted butter, divided

1 cup chopped white or yellow onion

1 cup sliced mushrooms

Salt, to taste

2 cups fresh spinach

1½ teaspoons dried marjoram

3 tablespoons all-purpose flour

1 cup milk

1 cup chicken broth

1 teaspoon dry sherry

Dash of ground nutmeg

1½ to 2 pounds skinless striped bass fillets, shrimp,
    or a combination, chopped into small chunks or shreds

1 cup grated Parmesan cheese

1 cup slivered almonds

Preheat the oven to 375°. Put a pot of water on to boil for the spaghetti. When it comes to a boil, add spaghetti and cook according to the package directions.

Spray a 9 × 13-inch baking dish with nonstick cooking spray and set aside.

While the spaghetti cooks, place a sauté pan over medium heat and add 2 tablespoons of the butter. When the butter is hot, add the onions and mushrooms, lightly salt, and cook, stirring, until they begin to soften, 2 to 3 minutes. Add the spinach and cook, stirring, until the spinach wilts, another 1 to 2 minutes. Transfer the vegetables to a large bowl.

When the spaghetti is cooked, drain well, then place in the bowl with the vegetables. Add the marjoram and toss to combine.

Place a saucepan over medium heat and add the remaining butter. When it melts, stir in the flour, then add the broth. Cook, stirring constantly, until the sauce thickens, 2 to 3 minutes. Stir in the sherry and a dash of salt and nutmeg. Remove the sauce from the heat.

Stir the sauce into the bowl with the spaghetti, then add the seafood. Pour the mixture into the prepared baking dish, distributing the seafood evenly. In a small bowl, stir together the Parmesan and almonds, then sprinkle evenly on top.

Bake, uncovered, until lightly browned, about 30 minutes.

Vacation Fish

When my husband and I take a beach vacation, we abandon computers and cell phones for stacks of books and beach walks. We stop by a fish market, grab whatever looks good, and never fuss over it. Truly fresh seafood doesn't need frills.

ALTERNATIVES:
whatever just came off the boat

Makes 2 servings

2 large, thin fish fillets
Olive oil
Salt and black pepper, to taste
½ teaspoon dried marjoram
1 medium clove garlic, cut into thin slivers,
    or about ¼ teaspoon garlic powder
6 thin lemon slices

Preheat the oven to 375°.

Place a sheet of aluminum foil large enough to hold the fish on a baking sheet. Place the fish, skin-side down, in the center of the foil. Shake a few glugs of olive oil over the fish, then season with the salt, pepper, and marjoram. Sprinkle the slivered garlic or garlic powder over it all, then place 3 lemon slices on each fillet.

Fold up the ends and edges of the foil to make a package, and seal the fish inside. Bake for about 15 minutes or until the fish is done. Gently open the foil to check for doneness, resealing if necessary. Pass the time while you wait with a glass of wine.

Hardy Plyler, Ocracoke Island

SAVING THE COMMUNITY FISH HOUSE

Finding the fish is one thing. A place to take the catch quickly for processing, icing, and sale is just as important. And in 2006, the last fish house on Ocracoke was set to close. Without it, the island's fishermen would have had to carry their catch to a Hatteras fish house, spending valuable time and costly fuel on a trip of several hours. (Ocracoke is accessible only by boat or ferry.)

Coastal fish houses have been steadily disappearing as development increases the value of the waterfront land on which they sit. According to North Carolina Sea Grant, 36 percent of the state's fish houses have closed in the past decade. Hardy Plyler and other fishermen knew that losing the fish house would be a blow to their work and the local economy. They formed the Ocracoke Working Watermen's Association (OWWA), sought out grants, low-interest loans, and donations, and purchased the fish house to run as a nonprofit. In addition to operating Ocracoke Fish House, OWWA focuses on education and research and serves as a voice for watermen on issues that affect them. Since then, Plyler and OWWA have talked to other communities about saving their fish houses.

Plyler, who has been fishing for forty-four years, says that fishing is an economic engine in many ways. "The fish house not only provides a place for fishermen to sell their catch, but it also maintains the fishing village image that tourists want to see. It benefits every business on Ocracoke," he says.

"What motivated us from the start is allowing people to make their living off the water as they've always done. Sometimes lines go out the door at the market with people talking about how good what they got last night was, and they want more."

Plyler's wife, Patty, is usually behind the counter at the attached market, where she'll sing the praises of sheepshead ("You can do anything with it") or explain why she can offer only head-off shrimp on a November day (at the end of the season, fishermen make more money on headed shrimp).

As Plyler waits for a load of fish to arrive, he watches the late afternoon sun over Silver Lake as sailboats return to dock. "Not a bad view from the office, huh?" he says.

For more information, visit ocracoke watermen.org.

Locals Seafood

Cajun-Spiced Shrimp

I have made this with butter and margarine, and margarine works best. Eat it with people who don't mind a spicy, messy meal, and have bread to sop up the rich sauce. The crab boil is usually sold as whole spices in a mesh bag. Cut it open to measure what you need straight into the sauce.

Makes 4 to 6 servings

½ cup beer
¾ cup (1½ sticks) margarine
2 tablespoons crab boil (such as Zatarain's)
½ teaspoon dried basil
2 teaspoons chili powder
3 medium cloves garlic, crushed
1 thick lemon slice
¼ teaspoon dried thyme
½ teaspoon hot pepper sauce (such as Tabasco
    or Texas Pete), or to taste
1½ pounds medium or large shrimp in the shell

Preheat the oven to 375°.

Place a large sauté pan on medium heat and add the beer, margarine, crab boil, basil, chili powder, garlic, lemon, thyme, and hot sauce. Heat the mixture until the margarine melts and it comes to a simmer. Simmer, stirring occasionally, until the mixture thickens slightly, about 2 minutes.

Place the shrimp in a 9 × 13-inch baking pan. Pour the beer mixture over the shrimp, making sure all the shrimp are covered. Place the pan in the preheated oven and bake for about 20 minutes or until the shrimp are cooked through. Stir once about halfway through the cooking time.

Carolina Shrimp Boil

Makes 6 to 8
servings

A summer day, cold beer, and a bunch of friends—that's all you need for this recipe. And fresh shrimp, of course. In South Carolina, they call this dish Frogmore Stew, but it's good by any name. Some recipes include smoked sausage, but I prefer the dish without it—feel free to add a pound or so of kielbasa, cut into chunks, if you like.

2 bottles beer (see Note)

1 package crab and shrimp boil in a bag (such as Zatarain's)

3 lemons, cut in half

4 tablespoons seafood seasoning (such as Old Bay)

½ teaspoon salt

2 pounds small new potatoes or red-skinned potatoes,
     cut in halves

1 medium white or yellow onion, cut into wedges

3 medium cloves garlic, crushed

2 to 3 dashes of hot pepper sauce (such as Tabasco
     or Texas Pete), or to taste

3 to 4 ears fresh corn, shucked

2 pounds medium shrimp in the shell

Melted garlic butter and cocktail sauce for serving

Use a pot large enough to hold all the ingredients. Place it on the stove and add the beer and enough water to come about ⅔ of the way up. You want enough liquid to cover the ingredients, which you'll be adding in stages, so don't overfill the pot. Add the bag of crab and shrimp boil and lemons to the liquid.

Bring the liquid to a boil over high heat, then add the seafood seasoning, salt, potatoes, onions, garlic, and hot pepper sauce. Reduce the heat to medium, cover, and simmer for about 10 minutes or until the potatoes are tender but not completely cooked through.

Break the ears of corn into pieces about 3 inches long. Add the corn to the pot and cook, uncovered, for 1 to 2 minutes. Stir in the shrimp and continue cooking for 2 to 3 minutes or until the shrimp are pink and cooked through. The fragrance will be a sign that they're done.

Drain the mixture in a large colander in the sink. Remove the bag of shrimp boil and the lemons and discard. Pour the mixture into a large bowl and let diners serve themselves. Offer melted garlic butter and cocktail sauce for dipping, and place a bowl on the table to hold the discarded shrimp shells.

NOTE: Use any kind of beer you have on hand. Omit if cooking for people sensitive to alcohol.

Christmas Eve Fried Oysters

Makes 3 to
4 servings,
including a
hungry neighbor

On Christmas Eve, fried oysters are a powerful draw. Once, a neighbor unexpectedly appeared at the door while I was cooking them. He loves seafood, but his husband can't stand it. "He's taking a nap. I have about 20 minutes," the neighbor said. I handed him the platter of oysters, and he dug in as I kept frying. My husband and I had always heard that a jolly man with a white beard would come to your house on Christmas Eve— guess it's true! Multiply the recipe to feed as many holiday visitors as you need to. Draining the oysters on a wire rack keeps them nice and crispy.

2 pints shucked oysters
1½ cups cornmeal
¼ cup all-purpose flour
¼ teaspoon salt
1 teaspoon No-Salt Cajun Seasoning (page 171),
    or to taste (see Note)
½ teaspoon dried parsley flakes
Vegetable oil for frying
Sassy Cocktail Sauce (page 164)

Pour the oysters into a strainer over the sink and drain. In a pie pan or shallow bowl, stir together the cornmeal, flour, salt, No-Salt Cajun Seasoning, and parsley. Place a wire rack over a plate and line a platter with paper towels. Turn your oven on to the keep-warm setting or very low heat.

Put enough vegetable oil into a heavy frying pan to come about 1 inch up the sides. Heat the oil to 350° over medium heat. (See "Best Basics"—Frying, page 16.) When the oil is hot, toss a few oysters in the cornmeal mixture and shake off any excess.

Place the oysters in the hot oil, making sure not to crowd them. Use a slotted spoon to turn them over to brown both sides. The oysters will take 3 to 5 minutes to cook, depending on their size.

When the oysters are lightly browned and crispy, remove them with a slotted spoon and place on the wire rack. Put in the oven to keep warm. Begin the next batch of oysters. When they're cooked, transfer the first batch to the platter lined with paper towels and keep warm, then put the second batch on the wire rack. Repeat with additional batches.

MAIN DISHES

Adjust the heat if necessary as you cook. If breading accumulates on the bottom of the pan, scoop it out and discard. If there's a lot, you may have to dump the oil and start over; the burned breading will cause the oysters to burn.

Serve warm with Sassy Cocktail Sauce.

NOTE: If you substitute a purchased Cajun seasoning, it typically contains salt, so you may not need to add salt.

Down East Clambake

It's difficult to give an exact recipe for a clambake because it's a use-what-you-have kind of thing. "People just show up at the shore and throw whatever they have in a pot," says Renee Perry of Salty Catch Seafood Company in Beaufort. "Grab some seafood, grab some veggies, throw them in a pot and steam, then eat." Some people include sausage, some don't. Some like bone-in chicken, while others prefer the convenience of boneless chicken breasts. Including sweet potatoes or rutabagas isn't unheard of. You can do a clambake outside on a propane burner or inside on the stove. The only requirements are fresh North Carolina seafood and good friends to enjoy it with. Based on Renee's ideas, I've come up with guidelines for a clambake that will amply feed around a half-dozen people, but add more of everything to handle a larger crowd. Feel free to experiment.

50 littleneck clams, rinsed well

4 ears corn, shucked

4 boneless or bone-in chicken breasts

1 pound medium shrimp in the shell

Salt and black pepper, to taste

Seafood seasoning (such as Old Bay)

6 small red-skinned potatoes, left whole

6 medium sweet onions, peeled and quartered

4 carrots, peeled and chopped into large chunks

8 tablespoons (1 stick) margarine or unsalted butter

Scrub the clams thoroughly under cold running water to remove any grit. Break the ears of corn into pieces.

In a large stew pot or stockpot, layer the ingredients. Start with the clams, then add the chicken, then the shrimp. Sprinkle salt, pepper, and seafood seasoning between each layer. Then layer the potatoes, onions, and carrots in any order, but place the corn on top because it cooks quickly. Sprinkle salt, pepper, and seafood seasoning between each vegetable layer as well.

Cut the stick of butter or margarine into pats and place on top. Add 2 cups water, cover, and steam for about 45 minutes, until the chicken and shrimp are cooked and the clams have opened.

To serve, use a large strainer or ladle to remove the ingredients from the pot, watching out for bones if you used bone-in chicken. Divide the pot's contents among serving bowls or place everything in one large bowl for communal eating. Offer the cooking liquid, now a flavorful stock, for diners to spoon over their servings as they wish.

Super Seafood Breakfast Casserole

Makes 10 servings

Potluck brunches are big these days, and a breakfast casserole shows up at every one. They're usually crammed with sausage and bacon, ensuring that between it and the Bloody Marys, you'll be napping the rest of the afternoon. This casserole has plenty of flavor but is light enough that you can plan activities for later, if you watch those Bloody Marys.

8 slices potato bread, cut into 1-inch cubes
4 tablespoons unsalted butter, melted
1½ cups shredded Monterey Jack cheese
2 cups chopped cooked asparagus (fresh or frozen)
1 cup chopped red bell pepper
2 cups chopped cooked shrimp, lump crabmeat,
    or a combination
4 eggs
2 cups whole milk
1 teaspoon salt
¼ teaspoon ground nutmeg or mace
1 teaspoon black pepper

Butter a 9 × 13-inch baking dish or spray with nonstick cooking spray. Toss the bread cubes in the melted butter. Spread half of the bread cubes in the baking dish, then half of the cheese, half of the asparagus, and all of the bell peppers. Spread all of the seafood over the dish, then the remaining asparagus, cheese, and bread cubes.

In a large bowl, beat the eggs, milk, salt, nutmeg or mace, and pepper. Pour the milk mixture over the contents of the baking dish, pressing gently to ensure that all the ingredients are covered. Cover the dish and refrigerate overnight.

Remove the casserole from the refrigerator about 30 minutes before baking to let it come to room temperature (it will cook faster). Preheat the oven to 350°. Bake, covered, for 30 minutes, then uncover and bake for another 30 to 45 minutes or until the top is puffy and brown.

Clams Peperonata

My friend John Barnum in Cary gave me the idea for this simple, summery combination of clams and sweet peppers. I used a combination of red bell peppers and red Giant Marconis, but be sure that any sweet peppers you use have ripened to red.

Makes 4 servings

½ cup olive oil

2 cups chopped white or yellow onion

2 medium cloves garlic, chopped

8 cups sliced sweet red peppers

1 pound chopped fresh tomatoes, or 1 (15-ounce) can
    diced tomatoes, with liquid

½ teaspoon dried oregano

Salt, to taste

24 littleneck or middleneck clams, rinsed well

Cooked rice of your choice or pasta

In a Dutch oven, heat the olive oil over medium heat. Add the onions. Cook, stirring, until the onions are soft but not brown. Add the garlic and cook for a few seconds. Add the sweet red peppers, tomatoes, oregano, and salt. If using fresh tomatoes, add ½ cup water. Bring the mixture to a simmer, cover, and simmer gently for about 1 hour or until the peppers are cooked down and are silky and tender. Stir occasionally. The sauce can be refrigerated at this point, or continue with the dish.

Pour the pepper mixture into a large frying pan. Reheat the mixture to a simmer, then nestle the clams into the sauce. Cover and simmer for 10 to 15 minutes or until all the clams open. Serve the clams with the sauce over cooked rice or pasta.

Easy Seafood Curry

Makes 4 servings

Fish and shrimp freeze well, and having a pound of two on hand means that you're more than halfway to a meal. This curry goes together quickly and can be as hot or mild as you like, depending on the type of curry powder you use, and how much. I prefer a Thai-style green curry powder that's moderately spicy.

2 to 3 tablespoons vegetable oil

1 cup chopped white or yellow onion

2 medium cloves garlic, chopped

2 teaspoons chopped fresh ginger

3 teaspoons green curry powder, divided

Salt, to taste

1 (15-ounce) can chicken broth

1 (15-ounce) can coconut milk

10 whole cardamom pods

½ cup canned chickpeas, rinsed and drained

1 pound medium shrimp, shelled, or 1 pound skinless
    firm fish fillets, cut into 1-inch cubes

2 cups fresh spinach

Cooked rice of your choice

Garnishes: coarsely chopped cashews, fresh cilantro,
    lime wedges

Heat the vegetable oil in a large, deep frying pan over medium heat. Add the onions and cook, stirring, until they begin to soften. Add the garlic and ginger, and cook briefly until they become fragrant. Add 2 teaspoons of the curry powder and a hefty sprinkle of salt, and stir and cook for about 1 minute.

Stir in the chicken broth, coconut milk, cardamom pods, and chickpeas. Bring the mixture to a boil, then reduce the heat and simmer, partially covered, for about 15 minutes, until it reduces slightly.

Add the shrimp or fish and the spinach, along with the remaining curry powder. Simmer, uncovered, for 3 to 4 minutes or until the shrimp or fish is cooked through. Taste, then add salt if needed.

Serve over cooked rice with cashews, cilantro, and lime wedges.

Crunchy Fried Soft-Shell Crabs

I'm traditional about soft-shell crabs, those coastal spring delicacies. I believe that pan-fried is the one true way to serve them—the crunchier, the better. As long as they're in the world, I'll never become a vegetarian.

Makes 4 servings

Vegetable oil
1 cup all-purpose flour
Salt and pepper, to taste
2 eggs, lightly beaten
1 to 1½ cups panko
8 medium-size soft-shell crabs, cleaned
Fresh Tartar Sauce (page 165)

Add enough vegetable oil to a large frying pan to come about halfway up the sides. Heat over medium heat. (See "Best Basics"—Frying, page 16.)

Place the flour, eggs, and panko in three shallow pans. Lightly salt and pepper the flour. Dredge each crab in the flour, then dip in the egg and dredge in the panko. Add the crabs to the hot oil; do not crowd the pan. Watch out for spatters as the moisture from the crabs hits the oil. Fry for 2 to 3 minutes on each side or until the coating is golden brown. Drain on a wire rack placed over a plate or on a plate lined with paper towels. Place the crabs in an oven on low heat to keep warm if working in batches.

Serve with Fresh Tartar Sauce.

Oyster Pot Pie

Makes 6 servings

Dale Curry is a former food editor for the *New Orleans Times Picayune* and the author of several cookbooks, including *Gumbo: A Savor the South Cookbook*. Dale branched out a little in the book and included this interesting and different way to use oysters. She says to use a double crust or only a top crust as you prefer. Thanks for sharing, Dale!

2 dozen large or 3 dozen small shucked oysters,
    with their liquor
1 tablespoon unsalted butter
1 cup sliced mushrooms
4 tablespoons vegetable oil
4 tablespoons all-purpose flour
6 green onions, chopped, white and green parts separated
½ green bell pepper, chopped
1 stalk celery, chopped
2 large cloves garlic, minced
¼ cup andouille sausage or smoked ham,
    chopped into ¼-inch pieces
1 teaspoon Creole seasoning
1 teaspoon Worcestershire sauce
2 dashes hot pepper sauce (such as Tabasco
    or Texas Pete), or to taste
2 tablespoons chopped Italian parsley
Salt and black pepper, to taste
2 piecrusts
1 egg white, beaten

Strain the oysters and pour the liquor into a large measuring cup. Add enough water to make 1 cup. Check the oysters for shell fragments and set aside.

Heat the butter in a small skillet and sauté the mushrooms until they are limp. Set aside.

In a large skillet or medium pot, heat the oil over high heat. Add the flour and stir constantly until the roux starts to brown. Reduce the heat to medium and cook, stirring constantly, until the roux is the color of milk chocolate. Add the onions, the white parts of the green onions, the bell peppers, and the celery and cook until wilted. Add the garlic and cook a minute more. Add the oyster liquor, sausage or ham, Creole seasoning, Worcestershire sauce, and hot pepper sauce. Cover, reduce the heat to a simmer, and cook for 15 minutes.

Turn up the heat to medium high and add the mushrooms and oysters. Cook until the oysters curl, about 4 minutes. Turn off the heat, and stir in the green onion tops and parsley. Season with salt and pepper. Cool.

Heat the oven to 350°. Place one of the crusts in a pie plate. Add the oyster mixture and cover with the top crust, crimping the edges. Cut several slits in the top crust to release steam and brush the crust with the egg white. Bake for 45 minutes or until the pastry is browned.

From *Gumbo: A Savor the South Cookbook*, by Dale Curry. © 2015 The University of North Carolina Press. Used by permission of the publisher.

Carolina Paella

Traditional Spanish paella includes mussels, shrimp, sausage, and chicken. My simplified version speaks with a Carolina accent, spotlighting the state's abundant clams. I used an aromatic rice grown in South Carolina, but any medium-grain rice will do. Use a large, wide sauté pan or a paella pan, not a deep-sided frying pan.

Makes 4 servings

½ cup olive oil

1 cup chopped white or yellow onion

2 large tomatoes, chopped

¾ teaspoon salt, divided

1 cup medium-grain rice

1 pound swordfish fillet, cut into 1-inch chunks

½ teaspoon crushed red pepper, or to taste

1 teaspoon paprika

1 cup fresh green peas

12 littleneck clams, rinsed well

¼ cup chopped fresh parsley

2 tablespoons chopped fresh chives

Heat the olive oil in a large, wide sauté pan over medium heat. Add the onions, tomatoes, and ¼ teaspoon of the salt. Cook gently, stirring occasionally, for about 10 minutes or until the onions are soft and the tomatoes have given up their juices.

Add the rice, swordfish, crushed red pepper, paprika, and 3 cups water, or enough to cover the ingredients (the amount will vary depending on how much liquid you get from the tomatoes). Season with the remaining salt. Add the peas. Place the clams in the mixture, gently nestling them into the liquid so that they are mostly covered.

Raise the heat and bring the mixture to a boil, then reduce the heat. Simmer, uncovered, for about 30 minutes or until the rice is cooked, the clams have opened, and the liquid is gone. You can gently shake the pan to redistribute the ingredients, but do not stir the mixture during cooking. Gently move clams if necessary to keep them in the liquid. Sprinkle with the parsley and chives and serve.

NOTES: Discard any clams that don't open after the cooking time.

The crust that may form on the bottom of the paella, called *socarrat* in Spanish, is prized. If you smell a toasty but not burned aroma and feel a little gritty resistance when you poke the mixture gently with a spoon near the end of the cooking time, you have it. The socarrat adds a smoky note to the dish.

Seafood Fried Rice

Fried rice is a good way to use up small amounts of leftovers. Consider this recipe a guideline for creating a meal from what's in the fridge. Chunks of firm, meaty fish or crabmeat would work as well as the shrimp, and diced carrots or bell peppers would be nice additions. Be creative!

Makes 4 servings

Vegetable oil

½ cup chopped green onion

1 cup chopped fresh asparagus

4 cups cooked rice of your choice

½ to ¾ pound shrimp, shelled (deveined if desired),
    cut into pieces

½ teaspoon garlic powder

1 egg, beaten

¼ teaspoon toasted sesame oil

½ teaspoon salt, or to taste

Heat a wok or a large, deep frying pan over medium-high heat, then add enough oil to cover the pan lightly. Add the green onions and asparagus, and stir-fry until they are tender but still brightly colored, 2 to 3 minutes.

Add the rice and stir-fry for 1 to 2 minutes. Add a little oil if the rice is sticking. Keep the mixture moving and don't let the rice burn or get crunchy. Add the shrimp and garlic powder. Stir-fry until the shrimp is cooked through, adding a little oil if the mixture sticks to the pan.

Pour in the beaten egg and stir-fry briefly to cook it, breaking up any clumps that may form. Turn off the heat, sprinkle on the sesame oil and salt, and stir to combine. Serve hot or at room temperature.

Shrimp and Corn Pie

Makes 4 generous servings

My copy of *Southern Cooking* by Chapel Hill's late, great Bill Neal has many dog-eared pages, and one is this recipe using fresh corn and sweet shrimp. The cookbook calls it a pie, but in the age of brunch, it makes a great breakfast casserole, too. Bill Neal would make biscuits from scratch, of course, but if you use an alternative, I won't tell. Frozen corn can work, too.

4 tablespoons butter, divided

6 to 9 cooked biscuits

1½ cups sliced mushrooms

½ cup chopped scallions

½ cup chopped red or green bell pepper

1 cup fresh corn kernels

¼ teaspoon white pepper

¼ teaspoon cayenne pepper

⅛ teaspoon freshly grated nutmeg

½ teaspoon salt

1 pound large shrimp, peeled and deveined

2 tablespoons dry sherry

3 eggs

1 cup milk

Preheat the broiler. Melt 2 tablespoons of the butter over low heat. Split the biscuits and line the bottom of a 9 × 13-inch baking dish with them. Brush the split halves with the melted butter and toast under the broiler until golden and crisp.

In a 10-inch cast-iron skillet or deep sauté pan, melt the remaining butter and sauté the mushrooms well over medium heat. Stir in the scallions and bell peppers and cook until just wilted. Remove from the heat and pour the vegetables into a mixing bowl with the corn, white pepper, cayenne pepper, nutmeg, and salt. Preheat the oven to 325°.

Toss the shrimp with the sherry. Beat the eggs with the milk and pour over the vegetables. Arrange the shrimp evenly over the biscuits. Stir any liquid from the bowl with the shrimp into the vegetable mixture and pour over the shrimp and biscuits. Bake in the middle level of the oven for 50 minutes or until the custard is set. Do not brown or let puff.

From *Bill Neal's Southern Cooking*, by Bill Neal. © 1989 William Franklin Neal. Used by permission of the University of North Carolina Press.

Sides, Sauces, and Sassy Goodies

》》

Asian Kale Slaw

Massaging kale . . . really? Yes! Gently rubbing the greens softens their texture and helps create an exotic and elegant slaw that pairs with many kinds of fish and shellfish.

Makes 4 to 6 servings

1 tablespoon sesame seeds

2½ tablespoons sesame oil

2 tablespoons apple cider vinegar

1½ teaspoons sugar

½ teaspoon salt

½ teaspoon black pepper

¼ teaspoon garlic powder

8 cups shredded kale

In a small frying pan over medium-low heat, toast the sesame seeds until lightly browned; do not burn. Remove from the heat and let cool.

In a small bowl, whisk the sesame oil, vinegar, sugar, salt, pepper, and garlic powder until combined. Stir in the toasted sesame seeds.

Place the shredded kale in a bowl and pour the dressing over it. With your hands, gently massage the dressing into the kale for 2 to 3 minutes, working to break down the tough fibers of the kale leaves. When ready, the kale will become shiny and begin to get soft.

Serve immediately or cover and refrigerate for up to 24 hours. Bring to room temperature to serve.

Classic Creamy Slaw

Makes 6 to 8
servings

Cabbage slaws often leave a pool of moisture in the bottom of the bowl. Salting the cabbage first eliminates that problem. You won't see a drop of watery liquid, even the next day. A creamy slaw is perfect next to fried fish or soft-shell crabs, or atop the Carolina Catfish Burger from Sweet Potatoes: A Restaurant (page 104).

10 cups shredded cabbage, at room temperature
2 tablespoons plus ¼ teaspoon salt, divided
½ cup mayonnaise
¼ cup sour cream
¼ teaspoon apple cider vinegar
¼ teaspoon black pepper
½ cup chopped red or green bell pepper
1 cup chopped carrot

Toss the cabbage with 2 tablespoons of the salt and place in a colander in the sink. Let drain for 1 hour. Rinse lightly, drain again, then gently squeeze small handfuls of the cabbage to remove more moisture. Spread the cabbage on paper towels to dry for 15 to 20 minutes.

In a small bowl, stir together the mayonnaise, sour cream, vinegar, remaining salt, and pepper. Place the cabbage, bell peppers, and carrots in a large bowl and stir in the mayonnaise mixture. Serve immediately or cover and refrigerate for up to 24 hours.

Spicy Red Cabbage Slaw

Abandon mayo-filled slaws for this slaw of a different color—and flavor.
Adjust the heat level to your preference.

Makes 6 to 8
servings

10 cups shredded red cabbage, at room temperature

2 tablespoons plus ½ teaspoon salt, divided

1 jalapeño pepper, sliced

2 medium cloves garlic

3 tablespoons apple cider vinegar

1 teaspoon brown mustard seed

½ teaspoon celery seed

⅛ teaspoon cayenne pepper, or to taste

¼ cup vegetable oil

2 tablespoons sour cream

Toss the cabbage with 2 tablespoons of the salt and place in a colander
in the sink. Let drain for 1 hour. Rinse lightly, drain again, then gently
squeeze small handfuls of the cabbage to remove more moisture.
Spread the cabbage on paper towels to dry for 15 to 20 minutes.

Place the jalapeño, garlic, vinegar, mustard seed, and celery seed
in a food processor or blender and pulse to make a paste. Add the
remaining salt and the cayenne pepper. Slowly drizzle in the oil with
the machine running until the oil is incorporated into the other
ingredients. Add the sour cream and pulse to combine.

Place the cabbage in a large bowl and toss with the dressing.
Refrigerate at least 1 hour before serving.

Sassy Cocktail Sauce

Makes about 1 cup

Making your own seafood cocktail sauce is easy—but if you don't include horseradish, it's just dolled-up ketchup. This recipe is from my book *Southern Holidays: A Savor the South Cookbook.*

1 cup ketchup or chili sauce

¼ teaspoon garlic powder

½ teaspoon Worcestershire sauce

Dash of hot pepper sauce (such as Tabasco
   or Texas Pete), or to taste

2 heaping tablespoons prepared horseradish

2 teaspoons fresh lemon juice

Combine all the ingredients in a small bowl. Cover and refrigerate at least 1 hour, until chilled. Stir before serving.

Fresh Tartar Sauce

Like cocktail sauce, this old favorite is easy to make fresh at home and tastes better than anything from a jar. Chopping whole dill pickles rather than using pickle relish gives the sauce a nice crunch. If you prefer a sweet tartar sauce, use sweet gherkins. Up the dill flavor by adding chopped fresh dill.

Makes 1 cup

1 cup mayonnaise

6 tablespoons chopped dill pickles

1 teaspoon grated white or yellow onion

2 medium cloves garlic, grated

1 teaspoon fresh lemon juice

Salt, to taste

½ teaspoon black pepper

Combine all the ingredients in a small bowl. Cover and refrigerate for at least 1 hour for best flavor. Can be made a day ahead.

N.C. Catch

WORKING FOR WATERMEN

The nonprofit organization N.C. Catch was established in 2011 to educate consumers, restaurants, grocers, and fishermen about the state's coastal seafood—how to handle it, cook it, and tell it from imported seafood—along with promoting underused fish species. The goal is to create appreciation and demand inside North Carolina for its own bounty.

"Much of North Carolina's seafood is exported out of state to northern metro markets," says Ann Simpson of N.C. Catch. "If you know you can sell the volume in New York City, Philadelphia, or Atlanta, and you're not sure you will if you drive it across the state, you're going to look at that sure sale."

The organization works with Outer Banks Catch, Ocracoke Fresh, Carteret Catch, and Brunswick Catch, which promote local seafood and recognize restaurants that serve local fish. The groups educate the public about how buying local seafood affects coastal communities.

N.C. Catch's educational programs for fishermen, packagers, and processors have covered aspects of sales and promotion, seafood tourism, and identifying new markets without increasing the pressure on fisheries.

In 2017, fish politics got serious. Proposed state regulations might drastically cut the harvest of the most popular seafood, shrimp, which is a big moneymaker for fishermen. The regulations might severely restrict consumers' ability to get North Carolina shrimp.

Seeing a need for increased awareness, N.C. Catch began offering public education about issues that affect consumers' access to coastal seafood. It encourages the public to get involved in those issues, which directly affect which local seafood you can put on your table.

For more information, visit nccatch.org.

Locals Seafood

Peach-Mint Salsa

Sweet and hot, this fruit salsa goes well on anything. Try it on grilled or poached fish or crab cakes, or add to a shrimp salad. If it's not peach season, use mango instead.

Makes about
2 cups

2 cups peeled and chopped fresh peaches

2 tablespoons fresh lime juice

1 teaspoon chopped garlic

2 tablespoons chopped red onion

¼ to ½ teaspoon chopped habanero pepper, or to taste

2 teaspoons chopped fresh mint

Salt, to taste

Combine all the ingredients in a medium-size bowl. Let sit at room temperature for 1 hour or refrigerate for 2 to 3 hours before serving.

Summer Corn Salsa

This salsa has plenty of flavor without heat, but chile-heads could throw in hot peppers. Top simple grilled fish with it, or use it in Grilled Amberjack Tacos with Summer Corn Salsa and Chipotle Mayo (page 90). If you have the grill going, grill the ears of corn for extra smoky flavor and let them cool before removing the kernels.

1 tablespoon vegetable oil
1½ cups fresh corn kernels (see Note)
½ cup chopped Anaheim pepper
¾ cup chopped white or yellow onion
2 medium cloves garlic, chopped
¼ teaspoon dried oregano
1 teaspoon apple cider vinegar
Salt and black pepper, to taste
¼ cup chopped fresh cilantro or parsley

Heat the vegetable oil in a sauté pan over medium-high heat. Add the corn, Anaheim peppers, onions, and garlic. Sauté for 2 to 3 minutes, until the vegetables begin to dry out and soften but not brown. Add the oregano and cook for 1 minute more. Remove from the heat and place the mixture in a bowl. Stir in the apple cider vinegar and season with salt and pepper. Let the mixture cool to room temperature before adding the cilantro or parsley.

Serve immediately or cover and refrigerate for up to 24 hours.

NOTE: If grilling the corn, you sauté just the peppers, onions, garlic, and oregano. If you would like a hotter salsa, add chopped jalapeños to taste.

Hot Pepper Jelly Glaze

Pepper jelly is the duct tape of southern kitchens. It can fix anything from a boring block of cream cheese to bland crackers. Pepper jelly also makes an excellent quick glaze for simply cooked fish. I like the sweet heat of the hot pepper version, but use the mild type if you prefer.

Makes about ½ cup

½ cup hot pepper jelly
2 tablespoons orange juice
1 teaspoon white wine vinegar

Combine all the ingredients in a small saucepan and warm over low heat, stirring, until the jelly is melted and the ingredients are blended. Keep warm until using.

Sorghum-Chile Glaze

Makes about 1 cup

Among southern sweeteners, sorghum syrup is often confused with molasses, but the two are different. Sorghum is made from a grass, not sugar cane, and isn't as bitter. Use this sweet-sour glaze on grilled or pan-seared fish. Be sure to let it cool a little first—right off the stove, it's as hot as tar.

1 cup sorghum syrup
6 tablespoons sherry vinegar
½ teaspoon ancho chile powder
Large pinch of garlic powder

Combine all the ingredients in a medium saucepan and warm over medium heat, stirring, until the sorghum dissolves. Simmer, stirring occasionally, until the mixture thickens enough to coat a spoon, 3 to 4 minutes. Keep warm until using.

No-Salt Cajun Seasoning

Use this as a rub for grilled fish, or mix it into batter or breading. It gives zip to Christmas Eve Fried Oysters (page 144). Be sure to use garlic and onion powders, not salts. Despite the presence of cayenne pepper, it's not an extremely hot seasoning.

Makes about ⅓ cup

1 tablespoon regular paprika
½ teaspoon smoked paprika
1 tablespoon garlic powder
1 teaspoon cayenne pepper, or to taste
1½ teaspoons dried marjoram or oregano
1½ teaspoons dried thyme
½ teaspoon hot chili powder

Combine all the ingredients in a small bowl. Store in an airtight jar and use within 6 months for best flavor. Shake before using.

Spiced Jerk Rub

Makes enough for
1 to 2 pounds of
fish or shrimp

This Caribbean-style rub brings heat and flavor to grilled fish. The heat level will depend on your choice of hot pepper. Try habaneros, Carolina Reapers, or scotch bonnets, or go milder with jalapeños. Use for fish steaks, whole fish, or shrimp on the grill.

3 medium cloves garlic, chopped

1 hot chile pepper, seeded, deveined, and chopped

3 tablespoons ground allspice

2 tablespoons brown sugar

1 tablespoon vegetable oil

1 tablespoon dried thyme, lightly crushed

1 tablespoon smoked paprika

1 teaspoon onion powder

1 teaspoon salt

1 teaspoon ground cinnamon

½ teaspoon ground nutmeg

Combine all the ingredients in a medium bowl and stir to form a paste. Apply a thin layer of the rub to both sides of the fish just before grilling. The rub can be made and refrigerated 1 day before using.

Crunchy Cornmeal Breading

Most purchased cornmeal breading mixes are disappointing—too much salt or just not fresh tasting. Make a batch of this breading while your oil heats up, or do it ahead of time and store it in an airtight container. Use it on fish or shellfish. The recipe can be doubled or tripled.

Makes about 1 cup, enough for about 4 thin fish fillets

1 cup cornmeal (yellow or white)
½ teaspoon smoked paprika
¼ teaspoon black pepper
1½ teaspoons dried parsley flakes
1¼ teaspoons salt
¼ teaspoon chili powder, or to taste
½ teaspoon garlic powder

Combine all the ingredients in a small bowl. Use immediately or store in an airtight container for up to 4 weeks. If stored, stir or shake before using.

Spicy "Hushpuppies"

Makes about 20

I put "hushpuppies" in quotation marks because some people will say that these aren't real hushpuppies but little corn muffins. But if you want the flavor of hushpuppies without the calories and mess of frying, these are barking up the right tree.

1 cup cornmeal
½ cup all-purpose flour
1½ teaspoons baking powder
½ teaspoon sugar
½ teaspoon salt
1 teaspoon garlic powder
¼ teaspoon cayenne pepper
2 eggs, beaten
½ cup milk
2 tablespoons vegetable oil
1 (4-ounce) can diced green chiles
Hot honey, butter, or cocktail sauce for serving (see Note)

Preheat the oven to 425°. Spray a mini-muffin pan with nonstick cooking spray.

In a large bowl, combine the cornmeal, flour, baking powder, sugar, salt, garlic powder, and cayenne pepper. Whisk to break up any lumps.

In a small bowl, combine the eggs, milk, and vegetable oil. Stir the egg mixture into the cornmeal mixture, and add the chiles.

Scoop about 1 tablespoon of batter into each mini-muffin cup; don't overfill. Bake for 15 minutes or until they are golden brown. Serve warm with hot honey, butter, or cocktail sauce.

NOTE: Hot honey is honey infused with chiles. Purchase it or make your own by gently simmering honey on low heat with a couple of dried chiles for an hour or so.

Crabby Bloody Mary

Makes about 6
servings

On an Alaskan cruise, I partook of a Bloody Mary that included a hunk of king crab. I figured Tar Heel blue crab would work, too. If you're not fortunate enough to sip this drink while sailing the seas, you'll feel like you are. Remember to purchase steamed fresh crabmeat (in plastic tubs) that is no longer raw and therefore safe to use in this cocktail.

3 to 4 pounds ripe tomatoes, or 1 quart pure tomato juice
    (no salt added)
¼ cup bottled clam juice
½ teaspoon Worcestershire sauce
2 to 3 dashes of hot pepper sauce (such as Tabasco
    or Texas Pete), or to taste
½ teaspoon prepared horseradish
1 teaspoon fresh lemon juice
Vodka, as desired (see Notes)
6 blue crab claws, cooked and shelled, or 12 large chunks of
    cooked jumbo lump crabmeat (see Notes)
6 large pimento-stuffed green olives
6 lemon wedges
6 long-stemmed fresh parsley sprigs
Old Bay Seasoning
Fresh lemon juice

If preparing fresh tomato juice, cut the tomatoes into quarters and purée in batches in a blender. Strain to remove the seeds, pulp, and skin. The tomato juice can be made 1 to 2 days ahead and refrigerated.

Put the tomato juice in a large pitcher and stir in the clam juice, Worcestershire sauce, hot pepper sauce, horseradish, and lemon juice. Stir well to blend, then stir in the vodka.

Get 6 long wooden skewers. Place the crab on each skewer, using 2 chunks if using lump crab, 1 claw if using a whole claw. Then add an olive and top with a lemon wedge. Put some Old Bay in a saucer and a little lemon juice in another saucer. Dip the rims of 6 tall glasses in the lemon juice, then dip into the Old Bay and turn to lightly coat the rims.

To serve, place a skewer and a sprig of parsley in each of the glasses, add ice, then pour in the tomato juice mixture.

NOTES: To accommodate nondrinkers, let guests add vodka to their glasses instead of stirring it into the pitcher.

Six medium-size shrimp, steamed and shelled, could be used in place of the crab.

Anthony's Oyster Shooter

Makes 4 servings

I told my hairdresser that I was looking for an oyster shooter recipe for this book. "Oh, honey, I'll tell you one right now," he said. He rattled off the ingredients while he snipped. Here's a written version, with thanks to Anthony Nance of The Elan Group in Raleigh. The shooters could be served as an unusual appetizer as well as a cocktail. Double the recipe for a larger group, and you can also omit the vodka.

½ cup vegetable juice (such as V8), chilled
½ cup spicy Bloody Mary mix (such as Zing Zang), chilled
2 to 3 dashes of Worcestershire sauce
½ teaspoon horseradish
Black pepper, to taste
Vodka, as desired
4 freshly shucked raw oysters
4 lemon wedges for garnish

Place 4 cordial glasses or tall shot glasses in the refrigerator to chill.

Combine the vegetable juice, Bloody Mary mix, Worcestershire, horseradish, and vodka in a cocktail shaker or small pitcher and shake or stir.

Place 1 oyster in each glass. Pour the juice mixture into the glasses. Garnish with lemon wedges and serve immediately.

Acknowledgments

There are so many fish in the sea and so many people to thank. I'll start with Ryan Speckman and Lin Peterson of Locals Seafood in Raleigh. They were a tremendous help with providing information, photos, and excellent fish and shellfish. Jill Warren Lucas tested recipes and patiently listened to my ranting, even as she became a grandmother while I was working on the book—you're the best.

Katie Mosher and others at North Carolina Sea Grant offered their time, resources, information, and statistics. Ann Simpson of N.C. Catch helped me begin to understand fish politics and connect with fishermen. Thanks also to Renee Perry and Steven Goodwin at Salty Catch Seafood in Beaufort for their time and recipes.

Several chefs were generous with their time, expertise, and/or recipes: Jason Smith of 18 Seaboard, Cantina 18, and Harvest 18 in Raleigh; Dean Neff of Pinpoint in Wilmington; Ricky Moore of Saltbox Seafood Joint in Durham; John May of Piedmont in Durham; Matthew Krenz of The Asbury in Charlotte; Stephanie Tyson of Sweet Potatoes: A Restaurant in Winston-Salem; Janet Lee of ZenFish in Durham; Keith Rhodes of Catch in Wilmington; Tim Coyne of Bistro by the Sea in Morehead City; Roger Hayes of WutYaSay food truck in Winston-Salem; and culinary instructor Amanda Cushman of Chapel Hill. Thank you to Susan Dosier and Jennifer Noble Kelly for connecting me with some of these chefs.

Cookbook authors Nancie McDermott, Ken Haedrich, Dale Curry, and Judith Fertig generously allowed me to include their recipes in the book.

Colleagues at the Association of Food Journalists offered considerable help and advice. The Southern Foodways Alliance's online collection of oral histories was a valuable resource.

Many thanks to photographer Juli Leonard for arriving for our shoots fully equipped with props and a great attitude. Cathy Hedberg, Jill Warren Lucas, Beth Langston, and my fish-eating husband Rob Vatz were intrepid pan-washers and onion-choppers during the shoots.

And I must thank the many brunch and dinner guests who were guinea pigs for recipes—especially my wonderful neighbor, seafood consultant and oyster lover Tom Attaway.

To my editor at UNC Press, Elaine Maisner, thank you for the gifts of your talent, flexibility, and sense of humor.

Index